Penguin Critical Studies

The Waste Land

Stephen Coote was educated at Magdalene College, Cambridge, where he was an exhibitioner, and at Birkbeck College, University of London, where he was the senior research scholar. Dr Coote is the author of critical studies of Chaucer, T. S. Eliot and English literature of the Middle Ages, as well as of biographies of Byron and William Morris. He is also the author of *The Penguin Short History of English Literature* (1993). He divides his time between a Dutch barge in London and a cottage in the Oxfordshire countryside.

Penguin Critical Studies

T. S. Eliot

The Waste Land

Stephen Coote

Advisory Editor: Bryan Loughrey

Penguin Books

PENGUIN BOOKS

Published by the Penguin Group
Penguin Books Ltd, 27 Wrights Lane, London W8 5TZ, England
Penguin Putnam Inc., 375 Hudson Street, New York, New York 10014, USA
Penguin Books Australia Ltd, Ringwood, Victoria, Australia
Penguin Books Canada Ltd, 10 Alcorn Avenue, Toronto, Ontario, Canada M4V 3B2
Penguin Books (NZ) Ltd, Private Bag 102902, NSMC, Auckland, New Zealand

Penguin Books Ltd, Registered Offices: Harmondsworth, Middlesex, England

First published as a Penguin Masterstudy 1985
Reprinted as a Penguin Critical Study 1988
10 9 8 7 6

811.52
ELIOT

The extracts from *The Waste Land*, *Four Quarters* and *Gerontion* are reprinted from *Collected Poems, 1909–1962* by T. S. Eliot, published by Faber and Faber, 1963.

The extracts on pp. 21–2 from *The Death of Saint Narcissus* and *Circe's Palace* are reprinted from *Poems Written in Early Youth* by T. S. Eliot, published by Faber and Faber, 1967.

The extract on p. 28 is reprinted from 'Ulysses, Order and Myth' and on p. 113 from 'What is a Classic?' from *Selected Prose of T. S. Eliot*, edited by Frank Kermode, published by Faber and Faber, 1975

The extracts on pp. 60–62 are reprinted from 'Tradition and the Individual Talent' is *Selected Essays* by T. S. Eliot, published by Faber and Faber, 1932.

The extract on p. 65 is reprinted from 'Ezra Pound. His Metric and Poetry' in *To Criticize the Critic and Other Writings* by T. S. Eliot, published by Faber and Faber, 1965.

Printed in England by Clays Ltd, St Ives plc
Filmset in Monophoto Times

To my father:
nil nisi divinum stabile est; caetera fumus

Contents

Introduction: The Collapse of Confidence, 1870–1920

The plunge of civilization u... this abyss of blood and darkness ... is a thing that so gives away the whole long age during which we have supposed the world to be, with whatever abatement, gradually bettering, that to have to take it all now for what the treacherous years were ... really making for and meaning is too tragic for any words.

Henry James

Henry James's despair was expressed in a letter the day after Britain entered the First World War. It was remarkably prescient. The majority of people believed the war would soon be over, and only after four years of incredible carnage (8 million dead, 25 million maimed) would those surviving come to see how the long, prosperous years of nineteenth-century progress had failed to contain the forces that wrenched them apart and left modern man broken amid the moral and physical Waste Lands of Passchendaele.

The Waste Land (1922) itself is, in some respects, a chart of this devastated world. Its rats and dead men, its arch-duke and talk of demobilization, suggest something of contemporary physical life, while its nightmare sense of collapse and fatigue, its feeling of the destruction of an entire civilization, is on a scale which only a truly world war could have prompted. To other men of insight, such destruction had been implicit from the start. 'I used to have strange visions of London as a place of unreality,' wrote Bertrand Russell of the early days of the war. 'I used in imagination to see the bridges collapse and sink, and the whole great city vanish like a morning mist. Its inhabitants began to seem like hallucinations...' Here, indeed, are the 'falling towers' and spent, phantasmagoric commuters of Eliot's poem. And, Russell adds: 'I spoke of this to T. S. Eliot, who put it into *The Waste Land.*'

But Eliot's sense of the collapse of civilization is far broader than the mental horrors and depredations of war. *The Waste Land* suggests something of its concrete details and a feeling of universal ruin, but the poem's concerns spread outwards to capture the moral, sexual and spiritual decay – the sterility and deep intellectual uncertainty – detected by some of the founding thinkers of the modern age from the 1870s onwards. These were matters that were to become more generally appreciated as the First World War and its aftermath offered massive proof of these men's insights. Fully to understand *The Waste Land*, it is necessary to view the work against this background of the widespread questioning of confidence, and the failure of science, sociology, religion, politics and the arts to provide a consistent metaphysical view of modern man.

Such a failure derived from the collapse of certainties, and those certainties had been, as James suggests, that the world was comprehensible and things were, on the whole, getting better. The basis of such a belief was science. Popular thinkers in both London and Berlin during the 1870s were agreed that, in the words of Beatrice Webb: 'It was by science, and by science alone, that all human misery would be ultimately swept away.' As a German contemporary wrote: 'Only in scientific research and power over nature is there no stagnation; knowledge grows steadily, the shaping strength develops unceasingly.' It developed, of course, to unparalleled destruction.

But there was a great deal that seemed to justify optimism: huge rises in the level of literacy, successes in the fight against disease, and, for a number, enormous advances in material comfort and some say in the means of government. Nonetheless, popular belief in the rational world of science and the intellect – the nineteenth century's inheritance from the age of the Enlightenment – was being questioned at its very centre before the outbreak of war. No longer could it be readily assumed that the methods of science would reveal an orderly universe and provide clear techniques for analysing man in a similar way. Physics, for example, was advancing beyond the stage where a simple mechanical model was sufficient, and the new concept of 'relativity' pointed clearly to the contrast between old certainties and new discoveries. Although so recondite a matter was unlikely to affect most people's 'commonsense' view of a simple world of cause and effect (it probably still hasn't) and although its relationship to the arts must also seem remote, it is worth remembering that when it was suggested to James Joyce (see pp. 27–9) that *Ulysses* operated in similarly relativistic ways, the author gave his assent. It was a parallel Eliot was also to draw.

While the idea that scientific rules are hypotheses rather than immutable absolutes – that they are 'neither true, nor false, but useful' – was being popularized as early as 1902, attempts to find scientific certainty in the patterns of man's own behaviour were being similarly undermined. Freud's epoch-making *Interpretation of Dreams* was published in 1900. The hostile reaction to his theories – his belief in the sexual basis of human motivation, its origins in childhood and its irrational, instinctual pattern – can hardly be appreciated today when such concepts are commonplace. But the word 'neurosis' dates from this period, and the ensuing vocabulary of 'rationalization', 'sublimation' and 'complex' points again to the idea of a fetid and unhealthy private world of frustrated energies that are too primitive to rise easily to the level of words. Freud would go on to develop such matters – particularly for their social consequences – after the First World War (which he saw as a huge manifestation of the 'death instinct') and give a more comprehensive picture of man as a sick, unhappy animal whose mental world rests tremulously on the edge of the dark. The presentation of sexual uncertainty as neurosis is clear in *The Waste Land*, particularly in the opening half of 'A Game of Chess'. Here, in the conversation between the distanced man and woman, the suggestion of a sexuality too complex and thwarted to find expression except in stress is strongly felt. That it was in some degree drawn from personal experience (see pp. 24–5) makes it the more poignant. Modern sexuality, Eliot shows here, is corrupted by forces beyond reason and is, consequently, sterile.

Philosophy, too, had been ousted from its position as the comprehensive expositor of reality. Just as the physical and psychological worlds had been shown by the methods of science to be less certain than had for a long while been assumed, so philosophy came to accept a severe fragmentation and the fact that it could no longer serve as a sure guide to values. Eliot himself, as we have seen, was associated with Russell, but his philosophical interests lay in different areas, and he was later to divorce himself from the philosophy school at Harvard – where he taught for two years – because he could not accept the separation made there between rational thought and religion.

Eliot's interest in philosophy had developed during his stay in Paris (see pp. 19–20) where, partly under the influence of French thinkers, he had come to experience a bewildering subjectivity in the world of perception. Some of the poems of this period – *Rhapsody on a Windy Night*, for example – document such experience, but Eliot's need to turn to religion is particularly interesting in the light of the work of contemporary sociologists.

Since the middle of the nineteenth century it had been hoped, in the words of Comte, that thinkers could go about the process of 'generalizing our scientific conceptions and systemizing the art of social life'. The result was a new field of endeavour: sociology.

The new science had to deal with two facts of overwhelming importance: a massive increase in the birth rate, and the effect this had on man's well-being. As more and more people were drawn into capitalist society and became ever more acquisitive of the wealth it might offer, so that society itself failed to provide the restraints and limits on the individual which could offer him a settled and reasonable view of the world. 'The appetites which industry brings into play,' wrote the sociologist Durkheim, 'find themselves freed of all constraining authority. This apotheosis of material well-being, by, so to speak, sanctifying them, has placed economic appetites above every human law.' The result was moral confusion: the collapse of known values and standards, a lack of acknowledged rules, and, as a result, the individual's crisis of identity in an incoherent world. It was a state which Durkheim called *anomie*, a form of rootless unhappiness that is clearly reflected in Eliot's poem.

Among Durkheim's proposed solutions was the rekindling of the mythic sense in man, an appeal to a higher set of values which would give order to (and thus contain) modern man's search for a soul. Again, *The Waste Land* derives much of its pattern from the fact that such myths had once existed, had welded the various parts of man's life together and so assured him of security, potency and a sense of well-being. Now the myths no longer function. Modern man lives in a world which, in the words of Max Weber, a second and perhaps greater sociologist, is going through a state of *Entzauberung* – literally 'unmagicking' – the disenchantment or disillusion consequent on western (and particularly puritan) man's over-rationalization. Weber, too, considered some functional substitute for myth and religion was an overriding necessity if society were to preserve a coherent shape.

But traditional systems of religious belief were undergoing considerable scrutiny, at least among intellectuals. The new interest in anthropology had revealed both the importance of belief in the maintenance of an ordered society, and also how allegedly more primitive people were able to elaborate highly sophisticated systems which took the instinctual life into account and provided the spiritual hygiene which the advanced technological societies of the west were corrupting. No longer could European faith – Christianity – be seen as a unique or even necessarily useful revelation. In line with this, the immense work of Sir James Frazer, culminating in *The Golden Bough* (see pp. 94–9), offered a picture of past faiths which severely questioned the unique dignity of the Christian religion and, sustained by ideas of historical development, could further suggest that far from being a special revelation vouchsafed to man at a particular moment of time, Christianity was, in fact, a successful derivative of much older cults. These cults, of course, play a crucial role in *The Waste Land*.

When we place such work as this in the context of the widespread assent to atheism among intellectuals (see pp. 85–8) – despite the almost universal sway of the various Churches' powers of moral and spiritual teaching among more ordinary people – then we can see how it posed a threat to traditional belief as powerful as that of Darwin, whose theory of 'natural selection' – free from divine or even human intent – had earlier swept the Genesis story on to the growing pile of discredited tales.

One further area might have offered a coherent metaphysical view of modern man: politics. The dominant political ideology of the nineteenth century had been liberalism, 'the belief that individual and collective happiness could be maximized progressively through the natural development of free institutions directly representative of the many who had some sure, and usually propertied, stake in society'. Such a doctrine of expansion and free enterprise had brought Europe (and particularly imperial Great Britain) untold power and wealth, but here, too, traditional beliefs were under considerable pressure, largely as a result of the massive rises in population which held within them needs and desires which the older doctrines of *laissez-faire* could no longer contain.

Such crowds had to be administered through increasingly centralized bureaucratic control. The enormous and seemingly continuous enhancement of state organization to which this led offered, on the one hand, a focus of power more concentrated than ever before and, on the other, a feeling of alienation and anonymity among the masses themselves. Here were forces for which new means of expression had to be found, and, in a world where the conventional restraints of religion were being undermined, the result was the powerful vocabulary of 'nation', 'race' and 'class', terms which could be given a coherence and dynamic – an ideology – far more telling than that of liberalism.

The search for an enhanced national identity was clearest in Germany, where increasing industrial wealth and the fear of encirclement served to stimulate traditions of authoritarian nationalism nurtured by the Prussians. Teutonism – the belief that the German people were destined to superiority at the direct behest of Divine Reason – became a major ideological force in sweeping the world to war. And the pursuit of such 'racial purity' is reflected in *The Waste Land*: Marie's 'Bin gar keine Russin, stamm' aus Litauen, echt deutsch' translates into the familiar racism of 'I am not Russian at all, I come from Lithuania, pure German stock.' It should be noted, too, that her childhood friends include an arch-duke. It was, of course, the assassination of Archduke Ferdinand that was the cue for the outbreak of hostilities.

By the end of the First World War another ideology wholly opposed to liberalism had taken root. At the graveside of Marx, his partner Engels had declared: 'Just as Darwin discovered the laws of development of organic nature, so Marx discovered the law of development of human history.' Here again is the rhetoric of a determinist view of man, a materialist ideology which offered an apparently coherent view of past, present and future. The vast numbers of the Russian proletariat had been vitalized to revolution in 1917 and, as the war came to an end, it seemed that yet others could be similarly inspired. 'The fear of revolution,' writes Professor Joll, 'was never far from the minds of the rulers even of the victorious countries.' The collapse of the Habsburg empire after 1918 led to a state of actual or near revolution throughout much of eastern Europe, and this even applied to Germany itself during the immediate post-war years.

Eliot was well placed to view this. He was working in the colonial and foreign branch of Lloyds Bank and, fascinated by 'the science of money', was helping with the pre-war debts position between Lloyds and Germany. He thus knew something of the financial collapse of the country – a highly revolutionary situation unsuccessfully exploited in 1919 – which had been caused by the punitive reparations demanded by the Treaty of Versailles. It is to such suffering and potential danger as this, to the force of the unknown revolutionary masses, barbarian in their new energies, that Eliot refers here:

> What is that sound high in the air
> Murmur of maternal lamentation
> Who are those hooded hordes swarming
> Over endless plains ...

That Eliot did indeed feel that European civilization was on the verge of collapse after the First World War is confirmed by Stephen Spender, who, lunching with him in 1929, asked what form Eliot thought the collapse would take. Eliot's answer was: 'Internecine warfare. People killing one another in the streets.'

On what could the artist draw to face these conditions? It is important to bear in mind that Eliot was an American (he became naturalized in 1927) with a broadly based European literary education and an interest in eastern religions. He thus had what Henry James saw as the American privilege to 'pick and choose and assimilate and in short (aesthetically etc.) claim our property where we find it'. Among the most fruitful hunting-grounds was France.

Just as other areas of European thought had drawn on the methods of science, so the writers of the 1870s, particularly the French, had advocated a 'naturalism' based on the close analysis of social cause and effect. Zola's novels – most famously *Germinal* – were the show pieces of the school. Naturalism also had its place in the theatre, and the result had been a widespread analysis of social issues by such writers as Ibsen and Shaw. But literature needs to draw on deeper imaginative resources, and the inevitable reaction to the naturalist school was the cult of aesthetics and decadence – the private world of sensation. The hero of

Huysman's *A Rebours* is a hypersensitive neurotic seeking release from the tedium of modern materialist life, and such an increasing subjectivity found its richest expression in the Symbolist poets. Rather than taking science as their model, the flow of language and the magic of words (the 'disordering of all the senses' as Rimbaud called it) led to the search for intuitive truths which the objects and events of the outside world might be made to symbolize. The world, in other words, was a metaphor; reality was an inner experience. To Eliot, the discovery of these writers – Laforgue in particular – was an artistic revelation of the greatest importance (see p. 20). It meant he could record the most intuitive shifts of the mind with a syntax and sequence of ideas that broke with the conventional lyricism of the immediate past (Hardy is a particularly good example of this tradition at its finest) while bringing into his verse ideas and images that the constraints of the older forms forbade. In such lines as the following, the very banality of the twentieth-century physical world captures exactly the horizons by which the poet must be bound:

> The bed is open; the tooth-brush hangs on the wall,
> Put your shoes at the door, sleep, prepare for life.

It is this technique which allowed Eliot to anchor *The Waste Land* in the concrete world of London commuters, pubs, the 'gas house', 'broken fingernails' and the typist in her bedsit who 'lays out food in tins'. Such things are at once actual and, in their very dreariness, a symbol of the dirty and sterile world that twentieth-century man inhabits.

The twentieth century is an age when the rise of mass population has led to a mass culture: the starvation diet of junk food and the junk novel. What did this leave for the true artist of the 1920s when the flowers of pastoral poetry had been squashed by the tanks, when the tools of the intellect had shown the world and the mind to have no clear rational order, and when the numinous had faded from the old myths of religion? The most obvious answer is sex. But in Eliot, Pound and, above all, D. H. Lawrence, neurosis, hypocrisy and 'mingy beastliness' have corrupted even this source of psychic vitality (see pp. 81–5 and p. 90–91).

If poetry, and the literary life in any sense, were to survive amid post-war ruin, its makers needed to salvage something for themselves, and there remained amid the detritus of contemporary flux the discipline, achievements and coherence of past literature – tradition, in other words.

The tradition of French poetry from Baudelaire and the Symbolists onwards had shown ways in which the ugliness of the modern world could be brought into poetry and so reflect modern man's position, while the technical excellence of their verse also set a standard of craftsmanship (see pp. 20, 50 and 109–23). To this could now be added those shining remains of more distant cultures – Dante, Shakespeare, the east and so on – whose importance became not so much a matter of dry academic inquiry as of urgent need. Here, in the great literature of the past, were things valuable in themselves and full of the richness of life. They could serve not just as tokens of better times, of past spiritual dignity and coherence, but as a means of measuring the pettiness of modern life and exposing its hollowness. It is for this reason that the works of Eliot, Pound (see pp. 89–92) and Joyce (see pp. 27–9) draw to themselves the wealth of past literature and, through parallels and contrast, through a continuous and sometimes tragic satire of juxtaposition, suggest a life richer than the modern world of sterility and decline. With coherence wrecked and confidence sapped, without a consistent and positive metaphysical view of modern man, a poet like Eliot, picking his way among the craters of a bombed-out culture, could at least declare:

> These fragments I have shored against my ruins.

The purpose of this book is to act as a guide to these, to elucidate something of the sources on which Eliot drew, and – far more importantly – to show how he used them to heighten the effect of his poem.

1. T. S. Eliot and the Path to *The Waste Land*

How unpleasant to meet Mr. Eliot!
With his features of clerical cut,
And his brow so grim
And his mouth so prim
And his conversation, so nicely
Restricted to What Precisely
And If and Perhaps and But.
T. S. Eliot, Lines for Cuscuscaraway and Mirza Murad Ali Beg

The Waste Land was published when Eliot was thirty-four. Behind it lay a strenuous history of intellectual, emotional and spiritual experiment, but only three years later he was to ask that no biography of him be written. The private details were not to be made public.

Throughout his life, Eliot stressed the 'impersonal' element in his writing, the idea that true poetry is 'an escape from personality' rather than an expression of it (see pp. 60–62). It follows that we must learn to see his work not as the outpourings of an overcharged soul, a revelation of the private experiences he was so careful to protect, but as a series of artefacts, well-made verses that communicate matured experience through a range of traditional knowledge. At first sight this may seem passionless. It is not. Under the prim exterior, the beautifully urbane manners, was a fermenting, deeply subjective man, fully aware of:

> The awful daring of a moment's surrender
> Which an age of prudence can never retract.

But precisely because such experiences are for all of us so very personal, their significance perhaps not clear until many years later, Eliot would have said that in themselves they are little capable of being directly analysed or used as the immediate subject of mature poetry. As we shall see (pp. 60–66), this in its turn had a profound effect on Eliot's idea of what a poet does, what a poem is and what both reader and writer derive from verse at all.

Thus, though the details of Eliot's life remain interesting – the details of a poet's life always do – it would be naïve to assume that they 'explain' the poetry. That poetry is, to repeat, a reinvestigation of the traditions of intellectual, emotional and spiritual life activated not by the scholar's desire to pin the past down but by the poet's need to find himself and belong to what he has inherited.

Repeated reading of *The Waste Land* will make this feeling clear. On a first acquaintance, it is a most baffling poem: disconnected, arbitrary, full of references and quotations not only in English but in a wide range of Indo-European tongues stretching back to Sanskrit. It is even supplemented by a set of notes. But in places it is instantly vivid and moving. The last section of 'The Burial of the Dead', much of 'A Game of Chess' and the central episode of 'The Fire Sermon' have an immediate impact. And it is just this power to raise feeling that urges us on. We come slowly to feel our way towards an appreciation of at least some of the powerful juxtapositions in the work and wish to understand more. We begin to want to deepen our experience of the poem by exploring its more difficult aspects. We shall find that if we do so by recognizing the emotion and drama of the supporting ideas – the sense of longing, fear and final triumph behind the vegetation rites (see pp. 94–9), or the ceremonious dignity of Spenser (see pp. 136–7) – then we shall not be hoarding intellectual lumber but acquiring things permanently valuable which confirm and enrich our first impression of the poem. It is for this reason that a lengthy account of Eliot's intellectual sources has been included here. These, as we have seen, are more important to the poetry than the details of his life. It is vital that they eventually be known and experienced. And it is our imaginative experience that is important – a response which Eliot's poem can deepen. Dante, Baudelaire, Shakespeare and the rest are not neutral clues in a donnish word-game but an essential part of our intellectual selves, the coinage of intelligent exchange. They are the foundations of the order and tradition within which Eliot worked, and they are a common inheritance. They are ours. *The Waste Land* presents many of them as something once infinitely valuable but now increasingly remote. If we bring our own experience of them to Eliot's work, however, we shall begin to meet him on common ground. In the end, Eliot's conscious reworking of traditional knowledge should lead us to read the *Collected Works* not as a diary or a cross-word puzzle but as a series of meditations. To adopt a title from his favourite, Donne, they are a record of 'the progresse of the soule'.

Having said this, it is clear that the aspect of Eliot's life which we must trace is the intellectual one: what ideas was Eliot nurtured among, what did he reject, modify or discover? This is also a means of approaching Shakespeare, about whose private life we know even less. A knowledge of the people to whom he wrote the *Sonnets* might be interesting – it would certainly have the thrill of good gossip – but it would add nothing to the stature of the poems, whose value lies precisely in their brilliant recasting of age-old themes into a timeless beauty. This is equally true of *The Waste Land.*

The tradition into which Eliot was born – in 1888 – was that of the high-minded puritanism of nineteenth-century America: bland, useful and, at its worst, rather smug. His mother wrote religious verse; his grandfather had been a leading force in the Unitarian Church. Poetry and duty surrounded his early years. So did other forms of culture. As a schoolboy, Eliot attended Smith Academy, where he studied Latin, Greek, English, History, French and German. He then went on to Harvard, a society 'quite uncivilized', as he was to call it, 'but refined beyond the point of civilization'. He took part in its genteel existence 'measured out . . . with coffee spoons' and, like his early creation Prufrock, wandered the slums as an antidote. He continued his studies in literature and added Dante to his repertoire, along with ancient art and philosophy. He also became interested in primitive religion and ritual.

We have seen that Eliot had begun to write, and it is clear from these early poems that, under the urbane surface, Eliot's spiritual instincts were deeply troubled. After a year in Paris he returned to Harvard with the drafts of his first great poem, *The Love Song of J. Alfred Prufrock* (1917). Here, in this powerful and remarkably mature poem, the precious, precarious social world explored by Henry James is threatened by intimations of chaos and extreme states. The balding narrator's cowardice holds him back in his boudoir existence, but the tension is there, an intimation of the opening lines of 'A Game of Chess'.

The Love Song of J. Alfred Prufrock (1917) belongs to the over-cultured world of Eliot's Harvard days, though its location could be any English-speaking upper-class suburb and urban backstreet. This is a poem about vision and moral turpitude, the fine web of social graces that binds itself round the narrator until the invitation to a rawer experience at the opening is lost in genteel tittle-tattle. The narrator cannot follow Emerson's injunction to 'affront and reprimand the smooth mediocrity and squalid contentment of the times'. Instead, the mild-mannered, balding Prufrock accepts his reluctant impotence. He can forge no link between the salon, the slums and the sea. He is no prophet, no hero. Caught in a polite, delicate world of tea and subordinate clauses, his vision of submarine delights is purely private, the fantasy of a fading gentleman. What visions he does have are of a guessed-at, but unlived life. He is the American cousin of the French Symbolists' sad dandy, particularly that of Jules Laforgue, whom Eliot had briefly sketched before:

... Life, a little bald and grey,
Languid, fastidious and bland,
Waits, hat and gloves in hand,
Punctilious of tie and suit
(Somewhat impatient of delay)
On the doorstep of the absolute.

The French Symbolist poets were of great importance to Eliot's development. By the time he came to write *The Waste Land*, he had absorbed a wider range of influences, but in 1908, when he first came across Arthur Symons's *The Symbolist Movement in Modern Literature*, he encountered an argument which suggested a way of putting spiritual vision before mere realism. The world may become – as Baudelaire had sometimes seen it – a 'forest of symbols'. All the things of the material world can, in this theory, be made into images of the inner world of the poet. We see this in such works as *Rhapsody on a Windy Night*, where the universe is an outward, visible sign of the poet's spiritual condition. Through it he can penetrate the mysterious world of emotional experience, explore it not always with hysterical extravagance, but often, like Laforgue, with a wry defeatism that is sometimes flippant, sometimes scathing, as Prufrock himself is.

Eliot had gone to Paris to become a poet. He returned to Harvard to study philosophy. His thesis work was closely concerned with the problem that was to preoccupy him throughout his life: the relation of chaotic subjective experience to a higher and absolute coherence. From this period stems the idea that the limited, individual consciousness is not reality. The matter is a complex one, and Eliot's use of Bradley (the philosopher on whom he wrote his doctoral thesis) eventually becomes that of a poet applying philosophy as a tone or colour to his thought rather than that of the rigorous professional logician. Nonetheless, it is here that we can begin to see Eliot moving away from purely subjective poetry and towards the communal, universal truth enshrined in tradition (see pp. 61–2). Some of the poems of this late Harvard period again show the religious tension that Eliot was experiencing.

Eliot taught for two years in the Harvard philosophy school, but, as we have seen, he came to object to its divorcing philosophy from religion. The latter was increasingly occupying him. He was now reading Dante again and committing long sections to heart. He had worked on Indian philosophy, in particular the *Upanishads* and the *Bhagavad Gita:* He was also reading widely in European mysticism and the lives of the saints. His Harvard poems reflect this. These later works are not as fine as *Prufrock*. Maturing is not the same as regular bettering. They are riddled with images of martyrdom and glimpses of divine reality, but they are not convincing. They discuss fleeing a world that has not yet been fully and agonizingly lived in. The great human strength of *The Waste Land* is the known awfulness of the real world. Its varieties of brutal deadliness have been felt along every nerve. In the Harvard poems there is only an intellectual position: sincere, no doubt, but thin and rather pretentious. Circumstances were soon to change this, and Eliot kept his early drafts. Several years and a welter of experience later, he was able to rework lines like these from *The Death of Saint Narcissus* more effectively:

> Come under the shadow of this gray rock –
> Come in under the shadow of this gray rock,
> And I will show you something different from either
> Your shadow sprawling over the sand at daybreak, or
> Your shadow leaping behind the fire against the red rock:
> I will show you his bloody cloth and limbs
> And the gray shadow on his lips.

In 1914 Eliot returned to Europe. The idea was that he should complete his philosophical education at Oxford. In reality, his strictly academic years were behind him. The young don with his intensely private religious life now met two crucial influences on the formation of *The Waste Land*: the American poet Ezra Pound (see pp. 89–92) and Vivienne Haigh-Wood, the English woman who was to be Eliot's first wife.

Pound was a brilliant sponsor of young literary talent, and Eliot was one of his finest disciples among the London literary figures. Pound set about grooming Eliot, concerning himself generously in the material details of his life and borrowing money for the publication of *Prufrock and Other Observations* (1917). Above all, he encouraged Eliot at this period to move away from purely religious verse and back to a satirical mode in which the influence of Pound's ideas is clear. Some of these, such as his anti-Semitism, are unpleasant in the extreme. The discussion of sexuality is also troubling and prefigures much of the analysis in *The Waste Land*.

Sexual inhibition – which is not the same as a lack of sexual drive – is clear in many of Eliot's early works. Something of this can be seen in *The Love Song of J. Alfred Prufrock*, but other and earlier poems show a fear of women, such as this rather Swinburnian stanza from *Circe's Palace*:

> Around her fountain which flows
> With the voice of men in pain,
> Are flowers that no man knows.
> Their petals are fanged and red

> With hideous streak and stain;
> They sprang from the limbs of the dead. –
> We shall not come here again.

In other works, such as *La Figlia Che Piange*, Eliot takes an alternative stance: the safe and melancholy delicacy of a moment which, for all its beauty of epithet, is again rather Victorian. The girl in this poem is less a real woman than a pose from a late-nineteenth-century painting. Thirdly, and perhaps more deadly, Eliot's women are charming but pretentious. It is these vacuous ladies of Prufrock's world, talking of Michelangelo, or the cloying artistic hostess in the *Portrait of a Lady*, who, under stress, lead to the neurotic, febrile woman of the first part of 'A Game of Chess'.

The fourth type of Eliot's early woman is the common good-time girl: the clerk's victim in *The Waste Land*, and, in such Sweeney poems as *Sweeney Erect* and *Sweeney Among the Nightingales*, someone more brashly vulgar and, to the poet, offensively sexual. Such are the girls in Mrs. Porter's 'rooming house', where Sweeney is a regular visitor (as he is shown to be again in *The Waste Land*, ll. 196–201).

If the women of many of the early poems are demonic or, more often, trivial, the women in *Sweeney Agonistes* say much about revulsion from physical love. They are degrading; and the degraded man is Sweeney, the barely articulate sensualist who says:

> Birth, and copulation, and death.
> That's all the facts when you come to brass tacks:
> Birth, and copulation, and death.
> I've been born, and once is enough.

Sweeney is modern, sensual man whose sexual instincts, though strong, cannot lead to a vision of an improved world. His interest in women is brutal, and the women he is interested in are low, tawdry creatures. Sweeney is no more than hair, eyes and mouth as he takes his vicarious pleasure:

> This withered root of knots of hair
>   Slitted below and gashed with eyes,
> This oval O cropped out with teeth:
>   The sickle motion from the thighs
>
> Jackknifes upward at the knees
>   Then straightens out from heel to hip
> Pushing the framework of the bed
>   And clawing at the pillow slip.

This is sex at its most empty, the degrading fear and passion that underlies the neurosis shown in such sections of *The Waste Land* as ll. 95–106 or 196–206.

The satirical poems which describe the collapse of European culture have great elegance but are riddled with disturbing anti-Semitism, a crude and rather sensationalist presentation of the idea that a Jewish economic conspiracy was undermining traditional values. This idea, as we have seen, may have been derived from Ezra Pound. A poem such as *Burbank with Baedeker: Bleistein with a Cigar* juxtaposes the cultured ex-patriot American, touring Venice with his guidebook and memories of Ruskin, with Bleistein – 'Chicago, Semite Viennese' – and Sir Ferdinand Klein, a womanizing financier. The confection of quotations at the start suggests the rich cultural past of Venice. The poem shows its collapse and Burbank's puzzled musings on this. This theme of bewilderment is suggested again in *A Cooking Egg*, while the impotence of the Church and its refusal to take a sufficiently radical stand on spiritual matters are hinted at in *Lune de Miel* and attacked in a more lively way in *The Hippopotamus* and *Mr. Eliot's Sunday Morning Service*. Again, the women in these poems fail to provide the prosperous, creative energy, the secure sexuality, which the poet needs. As early as 1909, in *Conversation Galante*, he had suggested that woman was 'the eternal enemy of the absolute', and this, of course, was to be taken much further in *The Waste Land* (see pp. 36–8 and 81–5).

The most powerful of these early poems is *Gerontion*, which Eliot at one time considered as a section of *The Waste Land*. Here a desiccated and empty little old man ruminates not simply on the unlived life and the decayed house in which he is living, but on the failure of spiritual experience, the triviality of those around him and his sense of being cheated out of meaning. There is a feeling of great age about Gerontion, of disillusioned passion and long patience, that characterizes some of the portraits of Rembrandt. Gerontion is more noble than Prufrock, more inured to suffering and disappointment. He is not at home in a salon world. One does not sense his wearing formal clothes. He lives among the detritus of time, in a world where 'Christ the tiger' is longed for by some, reduced to nothing by others. In the rhetorical fourth section – which shows Eliot's debt to Jacobean playwrights (see pp. 135–6) – time and history are seen as cheats. The great things of life are illusions which come too late or at the wrong time. Our motives are misunderstood. Love, despite being well meant, has been a cruel deception, and now 'I have lost my passion'. The aged Gerontion looks with saddened helplessness at the futile wreck of human life. He is a little apart from it in his sleepy corner. Such disillusion, the feeling that both private and public history had been a deception, that life is sad and unredeemable, prefigures *The Waste Land* even in its imagery. His moods are, as Gerontion declares:

> Thoughts of a dry brain in a dry season.

These varieties of anguish may be partly a reflection of the fact that Eliot's first marriage was a cruel disaster. To the shy and somewhat tortured don, Vivienne Haigh-Wood's vitality and lack of inhibition were perhaps challenging and exciting; but if we read the earlier poems to find 'the pattern ... of the personal emotion', then we come away with the clear impression that women's sexuality and his own response to it troubled Eliot deeply. He had been brought up in a puritanical home, he had lived an intense intellectual and spiritual life, and he was only twenty-six. A year after his marriage he wrote:

For the boy whose childhood has been empty of beauty, who has never known the *detached* curiosity for beauty, who has been brought up to see goodness as practical and to take the line of self-interest in a code of rewards and punishments, then the sexual instinct when it is aroused may mean the only possible escape from a prosaic world.

But sex was not an escape. Vivienne's mental and physical well-being were extremely precarious, and Lyndall Gordon comments well that Eliot's marriage – and with it the very poor state of his finances – was 'to be the grim underside of his life, the secret inferno to be traversed before he might be worthy of the genuine awakening only Christianity could supply'. A line of Eliot's own from this time is most poignant: 'It is terrible,' he wrote, 'to be alone with another person.' Terror and neurosis are the powerful subjects of the first section of 'A Game of Chess'.

The First World War kept Eliot in England. He was now living in a foreign country with an unsympathetic wife. He no longer belonged to the world of the universities. He had committed himself to literature and was still fervently searching for some form of religious truth. His conviction of man's corrupt nature had not left him, and now more than ever any form of tolerant liberalism was unacceptable to him. Poverty and overwork, first as a schoolmaster and then as a bank clerk, ground him down. And all the time he was reviewing and involving himself in criticism and lecturing. The pressure became intolerable and his energy gave way. He began to discover that suffering in unredeemed mediocrity is far more dreadful than the imagined martyrdoms of his early verse. Eventually he was given leave of absence by his bank and went first to rest by the English coast and then for professional help in Switzerland. He returned from Lausanne via Paris, where he presented Ezra Pound with the first drafts of what was to become *The Waste Land.*

2. *The Waste Land*:
A Description of the Poem

In view of the state of criticism with regard to the poem, it is best for us to approach it frankly on the basis of its theme. I prefer, however, not to raise just here the question of how important it is for the reader to have an explicit intellectual account of the various symbols and a logical account of their relationships. It may be that such rationalization is no more than a scaffolding to be got out of the way before we contemplate the poem itself as a poem. But many readers (including myself) find the erection of such a scaffolding valuable – if not absolutely necessary – and if some readers will be tempted to lay more stress upon the scaffolding than they should, there are perhaps more readers who, without the help of such a scaffolding, will be prevented from getting at the poem at all.

Cleanth Brooks, Modern Poetry and the Tradition

The Waste Land is a study of a civilization doomed by its own sterility. A chorus of voices, now individual, now subsumed in the blind and thwarted Tiresias, express wretchedness in their own or borrowed words. Round them the jagged memories of shattered past remind them of what they have lost: the potency of sexual and spiritual coherence. Precisely because they know only lust, neurosis or 'a heap of broken images', and because no one in the poem can patch these together, we should not expect Phlebas and the Fisher King, Adonis and Mrs. Equitone, to line up in a regular pattern, an order we can neatly explicate. Like figures in a nightmare, they are sometimes clearly themselves, at other times they merge into each other as tantalizing compound ghosts. Nonetheless, as we continue reading the poem, letting our intuitions strengthen themselves through familiarity and a knowledge of the text, so we shall come to see that Eliot's strategy for holding *The Waste Land* together is both important and interesting. It takes us to the heart of what he has to say.

Eliot's method is to juxtapose fragmented glimpses of the present – a moment in the Hofgarten, a visit to a Tarot reader, closing time in an East End pub, sex in a squalid bed-sit – with memories of the past. These latter are of two types. First, the positive remains of myth, religion and poetry which, in their fullness, suggest either ways of coherent life or the sterility of the modern world which has devalued them. Secondly, he uses moments, particularly from the Greek legends, which parallel the violence or impotence of his own time. In doing this, Eliot employed what, in his analysis of James Joyce's *Ulysses*, he called the 'mythical method'. Let us examine this in more detail.

James Joyce's revolutionary novel *Ulysses* was published – after great difficulties – in 1922, the same year as the *The Waste Land*. Portions had appeared in serial form over the years and, to the avant-garde, this novel by an exiled Irishman, published by an American in France, was a revolution in literature as much as in language. *Ulysses* was a European phenomenon, and serious fiction would never be the same again.

Eliot's review of Joyce's work, first published in 1923, leaves no doubts that he realized the importance of the book. It was he who had published extracts in 1919, and two years later he read the last chapters in manuscript. Both the technique and some of the details of *Ulysses* provided material for *The Waste Land*, and, while the degree of indebtedness may be a point of dispute, the analogies between the two (as with the analogies to Pound's *Hugh Selwyn Mauberley* [see pp. 89–91]) are useful in clarifying our view of Eliot's poem.

Ulysses is so vast a work that a useful summary is barely possible. However, since it is Joyce's use of myth that Eliot was particularly fascinated by, commenting on it in his essay in a way that throws much light on his own practice, some overall view of this aspect may be of help.

Joyce's novel recounts the events of one day – 16 June 1904 – and the lives of its two principal characters: Stephen Dedalus and Leopold Bloom. The first is a young man in the grip of personal crisis, an intellectual in need of spiritual rebirth; the second, a more mature and utterly down-to-earth man, whose unpretentious life eventually liberates Stephen's own humanity, artistry and emotional growth. But such an account, while clearly showing analogies to *The Waste Land*, goes nowhere to suggest either the breadth and focus of *Ulysses*, its closely rendered details of lower-middle-class Dublin life, its complex of internal monologues which recreate, with equal vividness, the mental lives of its characters, or the fantastic web of allusions to the sciences, parts of the body and, as its title suggests, Homer's epic poem.

It is by means of the references to Homer that Joyce relates his narrative to the heroic and mythical qualities of the *Odyssey*'s themes of wife, home, the bond of father and son, husband and wife, in a way that both draws an ironic parallel between ancient values and modern squalor, and, at the same time, elevates that squalor to show how there shines through it the eternal values of life itself.

This is at least part of what Eliot found so stimulating. He writes of

Joyce's use of the Homeric story as 'a way of controlling, of ordering, of giving a shape and a significance to the immense panorama of futility and anarchy which is contemporary history'. This is perfectly true, but the tone, the sense of doom-laden sterility in Eliot's words, does not quite correspond to Joyce's effect. Stephen (most critics consider) *is* redeemed. His contact with Bloom's humanity frees the artist in him. Joyce's vision is of procreation, the slumbering eternal mother-figure of Molly Bloom, whose relationship to her husband is also more or less revived. Stephen becomes more than the drunk young man outside the maternity hospital profaning the mysteries of procreation. But in *The Waste Land*, of course, such things cannot be. The women in the East End pub, for example, are squalid and infertile and no more than this. The women in Joyce's novel are much more fully conceived, much more than merely negative. Molly Bloom – who is certainly no better than she ought to be – nonetheless has about her the fecundity of the eternally feminine which Eliot's women deny.

Joyce's use of allusion, however, remains a matter of great importance. The use of Homer's story in *Ulysses* freed Joyce from the necessity of having to articulate a highly detailed story-line. The sense of narrative was implicit and already familiar from the Homeric story. The patterns and coherencies were there in the informed reader's mind. This allowed Joyce to make his points (if it is possible so to simplify his vision) by comparisons between his own characters' actions and Homer's, while, at the same time, allowing him to concentrate far more on the novelist's business of articulating his characters' mental and emotional states. And Eliot does the same. The religious mix of Adonis, Attis and Osiris, the plots of the *Aeneid*, *The Tempest* and the life of Tiresias, the subject-matter of Spenser's *Protholamium*, Wagner's *Ring* cycle and the medieval legends of the Grail, are all (or they should be) familiar to those who read the poem. These are what provide the narrative, the frames of reference, and they allow Eliot to get on with his poet's task of elaborating the details of the inner and sterile life of his times, the emotions aroused by his particular scenes. This freedom from having to tell a story and relying instead on the narratives of past myths is what Eliot means by the 'mythical method':

It is a method for which the horoscope is auspicious. Psychology (such as it is, and whether our reaction to it be comic or serious), ethnology, and *The Golden Bough* have concurred to make possible what was impossible even a few years ago. Instead of the narrative method, we may now use the mythical method. It is, I seriously believe, a step toward making the modern world possible for art . . .

It is at least partly by such allusions that both Joyce and Eliot provide order and form to their material and relate the modern world to the art of all time.

In sum, Eliot's use of the 'mythical method' meant that instead of having a plot or writing a narrative poem, he could dispense with a story-line and concentrate on the emotional significance of what he had to present in his various scenes. This could then be placed against the rich patterns of myth, worship and traditions of high culture which, lodged in the informed reader's mind, contain in themselves patterns of coherence and suffering against which to measure the sterile modern world. Eliot himself defined this process as one of 'manipulating a continuous parallel between contemporaneity and antiquity'.

For example, the vegetation and fertility myths analysed by Frazer (see pp. 94–9) provide what once had been a coherent pattern of love, death and resurrection. They gave the ancient world the magical, the potent and the sense of life renewed which modern man can no longer share. He, like Mr. Eugenides or Madame Sosostris, devalues and trivializes his inheritance. Death by drowning leads to a lovely moment of lyrical grace but not to renewal. Sexual potency is not restored, the numinous is not regained, and we are shown modern man living in a world unredeemed and closed to beatitude. By appealing to our memories of a sometime coherence in this way, Eliot's apparently disordered fragments of modern life become, as they are juxtaposed with it, all the more jagged and painful.

The same technique applies to the characters in the poem. These, drawn from the past and the present, from history, poetry and the imagination, are a remarkably heterogeneous collection: Marie, Stetson, the lady with bad nerves, Bill, Lou, the typist and the house agent's clerk, the Fisher King, Phlebas, Augustine and the Grail Knight are only some. It was necessary that if they were to be brought into the framework of the 'mythical method', some device be found to unify them. This device is Tiresias: the aged, blind prophet who has lived in both genders and in all times as a figure associated with death and sterility (see pp. 58–60 and 107–9). So amorphous a character can assimilate the others, as Eliot makes clear in his Notes.* They 'melt' into him (see pp. 82–5). Just as in

---

* Eliot's Notes to *The Waste Land* have added further complications to an already difficult poem. Grover Smith's use of them in *T. S. Eliot's Poetry and Plays* (1956) reduces the work to an anthropological tract, while Hugh Kenner in *The Invisible Poet: T. S. Eliot* (1959) tells us that 'we shall do well to discard the notes as much as possible'. The facts of their production are these. *The Waste Land* was first printed in the *Criterion* and the *Dial* without notes. Later publication in book form required the extra length they provided. Some of the notes, such as that to 1.68, are clearly ironic; others, such as that to 1.401, are useful, particularly to those without a knowledge of Sanskrit. Eliot himself declared that they were included just to pay tribute to Jessie L. Weston, but that he regretted 'having sent so many

Joyce's novel the events of the book can be referred to events in the *Odyssey* and the characters can be viewed both as themselves and as Ulysses, Telemachus and Penelope, so in *The Waste Land* fragments of action can be related to patterns of myth and culture just as the characters, while remaining themselves, can be drawn into Tiresias, the central figure of many myths concerning the subjects of the work. The timeless persona of Tiresias is thus another way of 'manipulating a continuous parallel between contemporaneity and antiquity'.

What follows is a close account of the development of *The Waste Land*, an indication of its argument, allusions and cross-references. It should be used as a guide to the text open in front of you.

The Epigraph

The first quotation which Eliot appends to his title page is taken from the *Satyricon* of Petronius (see pp. 129–30). During his decadent banquet and just before going off to visit his tomb, the vulgar and *nouveau-riche* Trimalchio describes how he saw the Cumaean Sybil suspended in a basket and being taunted by boys. When they asked her what she wanted, she replied that she wished to die. The Epigraph, which had not been Eliot's first choice, suggests the infinite world-weariness, blindness and absence of redeeming joy which characterizes *The Waste Land*. The Cumaean Sybil is the first of the thwarted prophets in the poem and, by having a figure from the ancient world comment in a manner that throws light on the present day, Eliot here provides an example of the technique which he will use throughout the poem. The literary nature of the work is thus made clear.

This is further emphasized in the dedication to Ezra Pound: *il miglior fabbro* (the better 'maker', or poet). This quotation is the first of many references to Dante and, while suggesting the enormous influence Pound was to have both on Eliot himself and the poem generally (see p. 89–92), it is also an indication of the poetic values of the past that are so crucial to *The Waste Land*. The phrase of Dante comes from the *Inferno* and is found in the context of a discussion of the troubadour poets of twelfth-

---

inquirers off on a wild-goose chase after Tarot cards and the Holy Grail'. Eliot never had the Notes withdrawn. It seems sensible to use what information they provide while realizing that source-hunting only serves poetry when it is the act of a cultured imagination seeking to deepen its experience of a poem as poetry. We might compare the Notes to a guidebook: useful, but no substitute for a visit to the place described, and something that eventually becomes redundant. This may also be the place to reaffirm that a first, unguided visit with ears and eyes open, responses alert and intuitions fresh, should make the greatest impression. It is the only worthwhile reason for wanting to find out more.

century Provence (see pp. 117–18), poets whose works deeply influenced Pound and some of which he translated. In their lyricism, cultural potency and celebration of love, these poets represent the origins of the great European traditions of high poetic art which go hand in hand with a refined but invigorating sexuality. The present-day lack of this is crucial to *The Waste Land*. Among other questions the poem asks is what can a poet do when the forces that once invigorated his tradition no longer have the power to sustain him. Pound himself had asked the same question in *Hugh Selwyn Mauberly*.

'The Burial of the Dead'

The first section of *The Waste Land* is rich, complex and widely allusive. It makes no concessions to the reader whatsoever. It presents Eliot's view of modern sterility on the widest scale and with the greatest possible elaboration of technique. The best way to approach it is to read it repeatedly, first noting its general plan, and then slowly building up the references until the whole can be grasped for what it is: a profound and very moving picture of modern man's spiritual plight.

The section opens with this idea of sterility conveyed through the painful imagery of spring (ll. 1–7). It goes on to suggest the state of Germany before the First World War and the spiritual inertia consequent upon this (ll. 8–18). Singling out the theme of spiritual death, Eliot then presents this in terms of the desiccated, desert world of the Old Testament Jews and their prophets, who, aware of the importance of spiritual life, have no glimpse of a redeemer. They have only fear and the dryness of their desert (ll. 19–30). This state is contrasted to a modern love-affair – beautiful but unsustaining – which is glimpsed between two snatches of Wagner's *Tristan und Isolde*, a work of throbbing passion and soaring love (ll. 31–42). In the next section, a representative modern man, anxious for spiritual guidance, visits a Tarot reader (ll. 43–59). Here we see how the once potent traditions of myth have been devalued and abused. Some cards, such as the 'drowned Phoenician Sailor', point to the man's spiritual plight and hint at redemption; others, such as the Hanged Man (which Madame Sosostris cannot find), indicate how blinded spiritual insight now is. In the last section (ll. 60–76) we are presented with this blindness on a generalized scale: the commuters of modern London are seen as the equivalents of Dante's spiritual dead in the *Inferno*. London is a version of Hell. The reference to Baudelaire (l. 60), however, suggests that London is the paradigm of all cities in periods of spiritual decline, and the concluding passage to Stetson (ll. 69–76) is a harsh challenge to rouse himself from spiritual deadness, examine himself and face the facts – face modern man's crying need for spiritual insight, religion and resurrection.

With this development in mind, we can begin to look at 'The Burial of the Dead' in more detail, developing its allusions and purposes.

The title 'The Burial of the Dead' is taken from the Anglican funeral rite and suggests, as the section develops, both the forgetting of an anguished personal failure in love (ll. 35–41) and the death of the once potent culture of myth in which mankind used to live. The survivor is the disinherited man – *El Desdichado* of de Nerval's poem (see l. 429) – whose barren, fruitless existence will be the poem's chief concern. But the title also suggests a third theme: the death of the divine but mortal lover of the Earth-Mother, or goddess of fertility, her subsequent withdrawal to the underworld and the period of agonized waiting while the forces of life are at their lowest ebb prior to the gods' reunion at the spring and the consequent resurrection of the spirit (see pp. 94–9). Such an event will not take place in the modern world. Though spring itself will indeed return, it will bring no joy, no rejuvenated soul. The myths have lost their magic and sustaining power. Man will be roused to the bleakness of his existence. Instead of hope, there is only continuous spiritual blight over the land, a blight at once physical and metaphysical which corresponds exactly to that inflicted on his lands by the maimed Fisher King of Arthurian legend, a figure who, Eliot believed, was directly analogous to the gods of the older fertility rites (see pp. 99–103). Just as the Fisher King's sexual maiming reduced his kingdom to a Waste Land, so the emotional maiming of modern man inflicts the suffering and death on his world that is recorded in Eliot's poem.

It is with this sense of spiritual anguish and decay, the time when death is so much more welcome than the first, painful stirrings of life, that the poem opens (ll. 1–7). To those inured to it, winter was the just-bearable season of a little, dry, warm life, defeatist and self-mothering. On the other hand, spring, the rising of the sap and the flowering of the lilac, is deeply uncomfortable: 'April is the cruellest month'. And with the stirring of life comes the revival of 'memory and desire', things winter had buried in 'forgetful snow'.

In the opening seven lines of the poem, Eliot creates a subtle and emotive suggestion of modern man's love of death and his reluctant participation in the rites of spring. The beauty of lilacs is repellent to him. Round their delicate loveliness coheres the symbolism of revival and memories of the dead (see ll. 35–42 and pp. 96–7), and these he would far rather forget. The brain and heart are stirring once again, but, in the clear parallel to the opening of Chaucer's 'General Prologue' to the *Canterbury Tales* with its exultation of budding April plants and love renewed, we sense how far modern man has gone in his longing for oblivion. The revivifying power of 'spring rain' is too painful for the moment. April here has no 'shoures soote'. Only later, as the great energies of despair in the poem are roused and the mind beats its desperate tattoo, will the promise of the black clouds over the eastern mountains (ll. 395–7) suggest the life-enhancing powers of rain and water, become signs of the baptism and resurrection that modern man so desperately needs.

By one of the abrupt transitions that are characteristic of the poem and which are a crucial part of its rhetorical structure (see pp. 64–5) we move on to a highly personalized memory of life in pre-war Germany (ll. 8–18). It appears at first to be a time of relative innocence and prosperity, of the refined boulevard culture of an older Europe. But if it is a time of rain and sunlight, of love, the exuberance of childhood and its delight in mountains and sport (compare ll. 331–58), it is also a period charged with hints of disaster: the racist nationalism of the old order who hurried the world to war on the assassination of an arch-duke (see l. 13 and pp. 9 and 13). Here we are presented with an elderly person looking back on this world. It may have left some delightful memories, but the psychological stress, the rootless dissatisfaction of life, are clearly marked in the last line of the section.

The second episode of 'The Burial of the Dead' is comparable but more wide-ranging. We move to a truly 'dead land' – the deserts of the Old Testament (see pp. 132–3). Here is a time without a redeemer and without symbolic water. The people have turned their backs on God, and infertility and destruction are the punishments for such spiritual blindness. This is the world of the prophets longing for Christ and aware of the religious barrenness of their age. In the punishing dryness of the desert (both actual and, in the poem, metaphorical), we see suffering and sometimes rebellious men who are aware of the vital importance of the spiritual life but whose crisis of faith in a time of the ungodly leads them only to terror, to the parched and vividly physical horror of 'fear in a handful of dust'.

This is a season which, like the present, lacks all sense of intellectual, moral and emotional coherence. Eliot expresses this in a phrase of crucial significance to the entire poem. In the dryness and sterility of their desert life, these men know only 'a heap of broken images'. In many ways this corresponds exactly to the form of *The Waste Land*, and it is the use Eliot makes of this incoherence, of the confusing inheritance of past culture, that accounts for the power, depth of analysis and difficulty of his poem. It is also the way in which he is most radically honest (see pp. 64–6).

One of the most vivid examples of this violent juxtaposition or parataxis in the poem (see pp. 64–5) comes in the ensuing quotation from Wagner's *Tristan und Isolde* (see pp. 125–6). We are jolted from the deserts of the Old Testament to the nineteenth-century German opera-house (ll. 31–4).

Tristan und Isolde is the apotheosis of late Romanticism, a music-drama of transcendent sensuality and death-longing which, during many stretches of its great length, is shot through with images of the sea as a symbol of passion. By placing his own description of a love-affair between the plaintive opening song (full of delicately melancholy longing and Celtic twilight) and the dying Tristan's knowledge of an open and desolate sea (across which, it seems, his redeeming lover will never come, l. 42), Eliot juxtaposes his failed moment of contemporary vision with the torrential lyricism of Wagner. The modern affair (ll. 35–41) has nothing of this fulfilment or tragic inevitability. Rather, though it is lovely, a matter of light, flowers and damp hair (all images of potency in *The Waste Land*), it leads to 'nothing'. The numinous fades, the mystical moment is not sustained, and its beauty is the more heart-breaking for being yet another incoherent experience in the great mass of 'broken images'. Modern love and sensuality have no power to redeem (see pp. 81–5).

The consultation with Madame Sosostris which follows (ll. 43–59) is important in a number of ways. It represents, first of all, the pathetic bankruptcy of modern life. Eliot probably derived from Jessie L. Weston the mistaken idea that the Tarot cards were used to divine the flooding of the waters that would redeem the parched Waste Land (see pp. 104–7). As such, the querent's visit to the card-reader suggests the feeble attempt of modern man to seek spiritual enlightenment. He will be bitterly disappointed.

But the Tarot pack does contain a rich symbolic suggestiveness and in using it (and adding to it where necessary) Eliot was able to introduce some of the leading images in his poem: drowning, the Hanged God and, more generally, the traditions of the fertility cults analysed by Frazer and developed by Weston.

Modern man has abused these, as the Tarot reading makes clear. Madame Sosostris's fair-ground name at once suggests this, while her false advice and the things she is 'forbidden to see' point to her as the wholly inadequate conveyer of the spiritual traditions of death and resurrection passed on by the Phoenicians and absorbed into Christianity (see pp. 94–103).

The querent's own card is 'the drowned Phoenician Sailor', a symbol at once of the fertility cults and of the people by whom such matters were spread. Now we are warned to 'fear death by water', the very thing modern man most needs. Already this card triggers thoughts of the drowned Prince Ferdinand (see l. 48 and pp. 138–40) and the rich sea-changes of *The Tempest*. Madame Sosostris also finds 'the man with three staves', whom Eliot associates with the Fisher King, whose maiming has brought a Waste Land to his kingdom (see pp. 99–100 note to l. 46). But with the mention of the Hanged Man (which Madame Sosostris cannot find) we are aware of the absence of a figure who – in Eliot's symbolism – crucially connects the fertility cults to Christianity and the tradition of spiritual redemption (see Eliot's and note to l. 46). We are left instead with the 'one-eyed merchant', later to reappear as Mr. Eugenides (see ll. 207–14 and pp. 41 and 84), and the hopeless crowds of the next section 'walking round in a ring'. We are left, in other words, without redemption or insight.

In the Tarot card section we see modern man trying for spiritual vision through superstition and being cheated even there. The traditions of faith are corrupted and inert. This state of spiritual inertia is also the subject of the last section of 'The Burial of the Dead'.

Eliot opens with a reminiscence of Baudelaire, a poet of the modern city and deep moral analysis (see pp. 109–13). He also closes the section. Between these two references (suggestive, on the one hand, of the surreal tableau of modern urban life and, on the other, of moral introspection) Eliot inspects his London commuters 'under the brown fog of a winter dawn'. Again, they are both actual and vividly located, while, at the same time (and developing the suggestion of modern man's search for coherence), they are the spiritually dead or blinded souls of Dante's *Inferno* (see ll. 63–4 and pp. 113–15). Modern London is thus trans-mogrified. It becomes the eternal type of the city of dreadful night (see pp. 79–80), a place where the masses of modern society ebb and flow in a godless, mechanical routine of work. War has led to death. (The battle of Mylae between the Romans and the Carthaginians in 260 B.C. suggests that all war is one war just as London is all cities, while, at the same time, pointing to the spiritual significance of Carthage [see pp. 96 and 127–9]). But the idea of resurrection, of the corpse of the ancient vegetation rites beginning to sprout, reminds us of the painful opening of 'The Burial of the Dead'. It is used here as a harsh and even abrasive challenge to Stetson, the representative commuter, to face up to the spiritual dead-ness that he tries to preserve in the unthinking hurry of his materialistic life. Here indeed is the modern world of godless, inert values, lost, hellish and sterile, which the vegetation ceremonies would once have redeemed. The closing quotation from Baudelaire, the appeal to rigorous self-examination, throws the whole into relief (see pp. 111–13).

'The Burial of the Dead' thus presents a view of modern man's spiritual predicament which ranges from the highly personal and specific, broadening through references to similar events in the Old Testament, pagan religion and the poets of modern Europe, to end in a challenge to face up to the spiritual crisis that Eliot has been exposing.

'A Game of Chess'

The structure of this section is not as complex as that of the first. Eliot is concerned here less to present a picture of the full range of modern man's spiritual collapse than to highlight the sexual and emotional aspects of it. In broad terms, he does so by juxtaposing the sterility of the wealthy and the educated with that of the poor and uncultured. Both point to the same end: modern man's failure to make sense of his emotional and physical needs.

The title refers to a play by Middleton in which chess is a diversion (as it is here – see l. 137) from violent and destructive sex in a world that has lost its moral bearings. The opening lines of 'A Game of Chess', which are a triumph of convoluted syntax, are also full of further allusions to Renaissance literature.

Starting with a reference to Shakespeare, Eliot takes Enobarbus's description of Cleopatra in her fabulous barge (see pp. 137–8), a picture of luxurious and exotic femininity, to produce his own version of what finally becomes claustrophobically artificial. This description culminates in an actual picture hung in the woman's room which represents one of the most violent of all Greek myths, the story of Philomela and Tereus (see ll. 97–100 and p. 131). The whole is a marvellous piece of artifice, a rendering of the unnatural and the cruel.

What is Eliot's purpose here? He has suggested immense material wealth, at first remote and heady, but, with the second sentence (beginning at l. 86), increasingly enervated. The words betray unease and artificiality: 'synthetic', 'troubled, confused'. Finally, the unnatural colours of the flames become a 'sad light' in which a moment from Greek myth, a story of rape, violence and attempted murder, brings the cruelty and neurosis to the forefront.

But there is the paradox that the metamorphosis of Philomela into a nightingale gave the world the bird whose 'inviolable voice' has always been the symbol of love and beauty – the core of lyric poetry. Now, in this time of sullied myths, her call is heard only as an invitation to physical sex (see ll. 102–3 and pp. 77–8). The 'dirty ears' suggest the mentality of the people who respond. The nightingale thus joins the other 'withered stumps of time', the modern debasement of ancient myth and

Renaissance celebration. The result is neurosis and suppression, a nightmare tension as the woman's brushed hair spreads out in 'fiery points'. No longer is there celebration or poetry. The woman is frightening and vicious. The staccato rhythms of her questions and confidences seem to pour out of her own emptiness only to fall into the man's vacant self-absorption. His mind runs on death and nihilism, 'Nothing again nothing'. He thinks of faint, painful images of drowning (l. 125), the sea-changes of *The Tempest* and the lost world of mythical death and resurrection (see pp. 139–40 and pp. 94–9), memories which take him back to the inconclusive moment of love in 'The Burial of the Dead' (see Eliot's note to l. 126) and forward to 'Death by Water'.

Here, then, is the world of anomic terror (see pp. 11–12) where the brittle, violent surface of the present can only sheer away into the horror of failed joy. Nothing, it seems, can relieve this stifled sexuality. Jazz might be a diversion (ll. 128–30). Rushing out into the street might be another. But sex and emotion have become forms of anguish, and this complex of sensations Eliot was brilliantly to define much later in *Burnt Norton* as:

> Only a flicker
> Over the strained time-ridden faces
> Distracted from distraction by distraction
> Filled with fancies and empty of meaning
> Tumid apathy with no concentration
> Men and bits of paper, whirled by the cold wind ...

The only diversions here are meaningless: hot water at ten (there is no suggestion of baptism or resurrection about them) and 'a closed car at four' in which the couple can avoid the rain. The suggestion is, for a second time, of the avoidance of the symbols of salvation that man so desperately needs. Chess is only a further distraction which, as the title of the section suggests, masks the barbarities of love-making. Narcotics, too, are a way out. The first clause of l. 138 refers to Tennyson's *The Lotos-Eaters*, in which men while away their time and avoid life's painfulness in a drug-induced haze.

But if futile and sterile sex, the collapse of the myths that brought joy and potency to ancient man, are the rule amid the fabulous wealth of modern society, so too among the poor and uneducated there is no sustaining sense of values. The proletariat offer no viable alternative to the decadent few. The gossip in the East End pub – its verbal patterns are brilliantly evoked – is vicious and demeaning. The 'demobbed' soldiers, far from returning to a land fit for heroes, come back to a London of women prematurely aged by abortions, their teeth missing and their friends hinting at affairs with their husbands. They look 'antique' in a world where sex is 'having a good time'. They are downtrodden and joyless in a life of drudgery that can aspire to little more than the philosophy of:

> What you get married for if you don't want children?

There is no sense of release from the crushing round of existence, here made all the more rushed by the landlord's repeated calling of 'time'. (Licensing hours, incidentally, were introduced during the First World War.) There is no culture here – the echo of *Hamlet* in the last line points to the unpoetic hollowness of it all (see p. 138) – and the overall effect is one of suffering amid gossip and trivia.

In 'A Game of Chess' Eliot produces a searing picture of the modern world of sex. Among the wealthy and cultured it has become debased and neurotic, among the lower classes it is a matter of abortions and promiscuity. Nowhere, it seems, is there a life-enhancing sense of joy, an access to the sources of healthy psychic activity. Nowhere is there a sense of redemption or potency. All is sterile – a Waste Land.

'The Fire Sermon'

So far we have seen Eliot present a widely ranging account of the modern world's decline into sterility. We have seen pained reluctance at the coming of spring, glimpsed the threatened pre-war world and watched the inert London of commuters, neurosis and the failure of love. We have been aware, too, of how Eliot has presented these against a background of searching spiritual experiment: the deserts of the Old Testament prophets, Grail myths, Dante, Baudelaire and the bankrupt tradition of vegetation and fertility rituals half glimpsed through Madame Sosostris's Tarot cards. In 'The Fire Sermon', which is the most subtle and comprehensive of Eliot's views of the modern world, both the observation of real life and the search for insight are raised to a higher level. This third section of *The Waste Land* is the one where the range of Eliot's techniques is, perhaps, most fully stretched. While this makes it one of the most moving parts of the poem, it is also in some respects the most difficult. It may therefore be useful to start with a general idea of its plan and development.

We begin with utter desolation, the decay and destruction of the landscape in which the Narrator (absorbed into the figures of Tiresias and the Fisher King) is left alone while, through his head, passes a kaleidoscopic range of references to the past: to Renaissance poetry (ll. 75–6, 183–4, 191–2, 196–7), death (ll. 185–6), drowning (ll. 191–2), Grail myths (l. 189) and sex (ll. 207–56). The last, whether the 'dirty weekend' offered by Mr. Eugenides (ll. 207–19) or the greater pathos of the house agent's clerk's visit to the typist (ll. 215–56), is sterile and meaningless. As these images pass, however, so there follow others of London, its glory and decay (ll. 257–99). None of them is coherent, and the polluted Thames drifts its way towards the Kent and Essex marshes until:

> On Margate Sands.
> I can connect
> Nothing with nothing.

The nadir of sterility is reached here and, with it, the violent juxta-position of St. Augustine and Buddha, the 'two representatives of eastern and western asceticism' (ll. 307–11). Some form of religious vision, an affirmation of faith beyond the harrowing details of every day, is called for. What we have been presented with so far has led to this need, and it is with the cry for religious vision that we move on to the last two sections of the work.

Such an account does not do justice to the subtlety of Eliot's presenta-tion of the Narrator, Tiresias. It is in this section that we first properly meet him and, as Eliot's note tells us, he is 'the most important personage in the poem, uniting all the rest'. It is through his eyes that we have glimpsed everything so far, and it is into him that the other characters 'melt'. In other words, the poem is his. A more detailed discussion of this may be found on pp. 29–30 and 58–60, while the literary and mytho-logical background to Tiresias is more fully outlined on pp. 107–9.

'The Fire Sermon', which provides Eliot's title to this section, was one of the Buddha's first expressions of the fruits of his enlightenment. In it he takes fire as a symbol of desire (see pp. 119–20): desire not just for sex, but for any form of attachment to worldly things. Such burning with need binds man for ever to the wheel of cause and effect and hence forbids him any means of liberation or happiness. It is with this idea in mind – the basic philosophy of Buddhism – that we should read this section of the poem.

'The Fire Sermon' begins with a description of an actual Waste Land, a brown and leafless desert swept by the wind. The wet banks of the river can no longer be thought of as the Thames in its Renaissance glory (see pp. 136–7). Here is not the place for the celebration of marriage, of sexual and cultural potency (ll. 176, 179, 183–4), and this is painful to the narrating Tiresias, who is left alone without even the modern secretaries and their bosses who have replaced Spenser's nymphs (ll. 179–81). In his loneliness, he becomes both the psalmist weeping by Zion (l. 192) and (possibly) Eliot himself remembering his cure for nervous disorders in Switzerland (see pp. 24–5). (Leman is the Swiss name for Lake Geneva.) The painful contrast suggested by the Spenser poem is repeated (ll. 183–4), but its hushed beauty is broken by a reference to Marvell's *To His Coy Mistress* with its impression of time the destroyer and death the inevitable end of life (see l. 185 and p. 136). The references to seventeenth-century English literature all the way through the poem constantly vary between the beautiful, as in the Spenser allusions, and the sinister, as here.

Lingering by the water in this way, 'fishing in the dull canal', the Narrator becomes absorbed into the figure of the Fisher King from the Arthurian legends (see pp. 99–101), who, with his deep physical and psychic wound, has inflicted on his kingdom the sterile blight which makes it a Waste Land. We are referred again to the world of myth and to the absorption of the ancient fertility rituals into the Christianized legends of the Middle Ages. What we are presented with here is a period of mourning and sterility, of the impotence of the world in the absence of a redeeming spirit. This is a period not simply of physical but also of emotional and intellectual collapse. All that Tiresias – his existence stretched across time – can think of is the memory of another drowning, that mentioned in *The Tempest* (see ll. 191–2 and pp. 138–40), which leads to the sea-changes and moral transformations of the erring characters in the play. Again, this refers us back to the wretched lover in the first part of 'A Game of Chess' (ll. 124–5), the man (at once himself and Tiresias) who, in his chronic isolation, can only let his suffering mind run on images at once of beauty and destruction which now no longer prefigure a resurrection and a new life. Instead there is only death:

> . . . bones cast in a little low dry garret
> Rattled by the rat's foot only, year to year.

It is with these creatures (familiar from the First World War) that the second part of 'The Fire Sermon' opens (ll. 187–202). We have been forced to view a world of corruption and decay, a sterility which is, as the next lines (ll. 196–201) show us, not merely a matter of mourning for past and lost ideas of redemption, but of the active wretchedness of modern, sensual man. He is personified in Sweeney on his way to visit Mrs. Porter's brothel (see pp. 22–3 and 81–2). Here is modern physical life at its lowest, and in his attempt to juxtapose it with the past, Eliot refers first to a seventeenth-century working of the myth of Diana and Actaeon (see l. 197, Eliot's note) and then to ballad poetry, which has here a sense of 'low life' and cultural banality (ll. 199–201). In Sweeney and the women, the lumpishly physical is triumphant and sex is a form of brutality. This latter is made clear by the contrast to the ensuing quotation from Verlaine's *Parsifal* (l. 202), a poem in which the triumph of the young and virgin knight over his boy's desire and over the chattering, diverting lust roused by young girls has allowed him to penetrate the mysteries of the Grail, heal the Fisher King and replace him in the castle as the high priest of the sacred mysteries. It is these rites which represent the triumph of the spiritual over the fleshly, of the religious life over the physical, and, hence, the redemption of the Waste Land of sexual impurity. It is the rites of the Grail chapel in the redeemed Waste Land, rites that took place after a ceremonial washing of feet parodied in the Mrs. Porter lines, that are accompanied by the 'voices of children chanting in the choir'. To the Narrator, these are a vision remembered only in poetry, and they form a bitter contrast to the world of everyday lust, the violence and the nausea that accompany memories of the myth of Tereus (l. 206) alluded to in 'A Game of Chess', the rape and subsequent corruption of lyric poetry by the crude, modern insistence on 'Jug, jug' (see ll. 97–103).

This world of unrelieved sexual grossness now becomes Eliot's theme. In the lines of bird song (ll. 203–4), passages from earlier in the poem have been re-used and broadened in their significance (see pp. 77–8). In the section on Mr. Eugenides that follows (ll. 207–14), the first line refers us back to 'The Burial of the Dead' and the vision in the last section of that, in which London became the archetype of the unredeemed city of dreadful night – a horrific, almost surreal stage (l. 60). It becomes so again; but, instead of a place where moral earnestness can at least be suggested, it is now the place where myth becomes most corrupted.

Mr. Eugenides (his name means 'the well-born') tries to seduce the Narrator with promises of lunch and a dirty weekend in Brighton. The fog hangs over the scene just as it did in 'The Burial of the Dead' and suggests corruption and obscurity. Mr. Eugenides's name and his place of birth, on the other hand, suggest the far-different worlds of cultural and spiritual affirmation that had once existed when the fertility myths had given man hope and coherence. Now they are horribly degraded by this one-eyed (in other words, all-but-blinded) merchant whom we first glimpsed in Madame Sosostris's Tarot pack (ll. 52–3) and who now, instead of offering rapture and fulfilment, insight and potency, can only suggest something as squalid as Sweeney and Mrs. Porter or the scene of joyless sexuality that follows (ll. 215–56).

The myths have been abused. Man has turned his back on the spiritual and is unable to glimpse the means of his redemption. He is lost, squalid and desperate in a world where sex is devalued and meaningless. Swept up by a lust which has neither dignity nor purpose, and wretchedly inhabiting a materialistic world that demeans the individual and makes a mockery of the cultural values of the past, modern life and love can be nothing more than the selfish and miserable conquest by the acne-covered clerk of the slatternly typist.

These lines (ll. 215–58) are some of the most powerful in the whole of Eliot's work. The sheer unpleasantness of what they describe could easily have become a form of sentimentality, but the strict control of the verse form (and hence its ironic gesture towards order and beauty) and the precision with which the physical world is observed combine with the figure of Tiresias (fully introduced here for the first time) to capture perfectly the impotent and pathetic world that is the subject of Eliot's poem. Here is an action at once contemporary and ageless, suggesting both revulsion and pity.

After the seduction, the music from the 'gramophone' ironically reminds Tiresias of *The Tempest*, of Ariel and of salvation through drowning (l. 257). Once more we are in a world of water and memories of the Fisher King. We are also in London and, through the imagery of 'fishermen', the area around Billingsgate (l. 260) and its church of Magnus Martyr (see pp. 78–9). We see the city both in itself and in terms of the fishing symbolism (see pp. 76–7 and 100) and of ideas of religion and spiritual values which once existed as pledges of potency and which are still enshrined in the church's

Inexplicable splendour of Ionian white and gold.

But the vision cannot last for long. The Thames is other things besides references to these myths. The river becomes, for example, the Rhine of Wagner's *Twilight of the Gods* (see p. 126 and Eliot's note to l. 266). As the river flows out of the City, so its varying history is recounted through an allusion to the Rhinemaidens lamenting the theft of their gold and the sadness of their river now that it has lost its primal innocence. It is through the theft of this gold that both men and the gods are hastening their own ruin (ll. 266–99).

We see, first of all, the present-day Thames itself, dirty but still mildly romantic (ll. 266–78). We then see it in the days of Elizabeth and Leicester – the period of Spenser, too – glorious but, even here, futile in its pageantry (see ll. 279–91 and Eliot's note to l. 279). Finally, as it flows further on, the unhappiness of modern lovers with their fractured relationships and promises of 'a new start' come into the foreground, until, in the section beginning at l. 300, there is only nihilism. Nothing connects. The world has lost its coherence, is impotent, dirty and meaningless. We end up on the sterile sand at Margate, and become like the Old Testament prophets in their deserts in 'The Burial of the

Dead'. Like them, the Narrator knows only 'a heap of broken images'. Here, indeed, is the Waste Land at the core of modern life: inert, spiritually dead, sexually wretched.

To such does desire lead: not to happiness or fulfilment, but to the wretchedness of modern lust, the discovery of the corrupt city of man that St. Augustine made in his early youth and recorded in his *Confessions* (see pp. 127–9). The 'unholy loves of Carthage' are painful and untrue since they are not directed to God. 'But I deserted you, my God. In my youth I wandered away too far from your sustaining hand, and created of myself a barren waste.' St. Augustine's vision here is of the inner burning desert of the soul, lusting but sterile. Man is aflame with desire, but such desire leads only to the discovery of psychological and spiritual death. From such he must be redeemed. Such, too, is the teaching of the Buddha. It is at this point (ll. 307–11) that Eliot makes his 'collocation of these two representatives of eastern and western asceticism'. Although widely different in crucial ways, both Buddha (see pp. 119–20), and St. Augustine (see pp. 127–9) were concerned to find a final peace and, in their withdrawal from the world of sensual desire, agreed in the need for a vision beyond the world of purely human emotion.

'Death by Water'

The querent at Madame Sosostris's Tarot reading (l. 55) has been told to 'fear death by water'. The warning symbolizes contemporary spiritual blindness since, in the ancient cults, this form of death was a prelude to resurrection and the renewal of the fertility of the land (see pp. 95–6). As we have seen, these myths are no longer potent, but here even a memory of them provides a brief but lyrical interlude somewhat akin to similar lyrics in *The Greek Anthology* (see p. 132).

Eliot comments that 'The one-eyed merchant, seller of currants, melts into the Phoenician Sailor, and the latter is not wholly distinct from Ferdinand Prince of Naples'. In other words, the images of drowning devalued by the modern world, especially by Mr. Eugenides, here combine with memories of the sea-change of *The Tempest* recalled by the anguished man in 'A Game of Chess' (l. 125) and by the narrating Tiresias in 'The Fire Sermon' (ll. 191–2). Throughout, they have been a reminder of better and more potent times. Now, if they cannot transfigure the Waste Land, they can at least provide an appealing and gentle sense of loss and annihilation – even of Mr. Eugenides – which will lead, if not to resurrection, then at least to the heightened spiritual insight of 'What the Thunder said'.

'What the Thunder said'

The title again refers us to eastern religion; not, this time, to the insights of the Buddha, but to the moral guidance offered by the Hindu *Brihadaranyaka Upanishad*. Here is a vision of freedom beyond the constraints of desire and one which is connected, as it happens, to ideas of rain and fertility (see pp. 121–3). The suggestion in this Hindu gospel is that through 'right action' – giving, sympathy and self-control – man may indeed go beyond his sterile world and hence revive the potency of the universe in which he lives.

Again, since 'What the Thunder said' is a complex passage, some idea of its overall plan will be useful.

We begin in the world of the slaughtered god and the consequent period of mourning and infertility prior to his resurrection (ll. 322–94). On this occasion Eliot takes Christ as his representative deity, and glimpses of Gethsemane and the trial before Pilate are juxtaposed with images of spiritual death (ll. 322–6). In the next section (ll. 331–58) these images of spiritual death are developed to present a barren, mountainous world, a waterless landscape of rock and sand far from Marie's childhood delights (compare ll. 8–18) and much closer to the deserts of the Old Testament prophets (see pp. 33 and 132–3). Here is a purgatory where physical and emotional discomfort are united. There is no rest here and no silence. Diabolic faces 'sneer and snarl' while all around is the rumble of 'dry sterile thunder without rain'. This is a place of nightmare extremes and the mind at the end of its tether, its pains worsened by the teasing song of the hermit-thrush (see ll. 356–75 and p. 78).

And even when the god has risen, man cannot recognize him. In the fourth section (ll. 359–65), developing the Christian imagery of the first (ll. 322–30), Eliot presents the biblical story of the appearance of Jesus to his disciples on the road to Emmaus (see pp. 134–5). Believing that their saviour has left them, the disciples are so confused that, when the resurrected Christ does indeed return to them, they cannot recognize him. Only when he has gone again do they realize what has happened. Man's access to the world of the spirit is not automatic or immediately comprehending. But it is important to remember that at this stage Eliot was not a fully professed Christian and, building on the ideas suggested to him by *The Golden Bough*, he merges the image of Christ with an analogous deity, Frazer's Hanged God, whom, as the Notes tell us, he associated with 'the hooded figure in the passage of the disciples of Emmaus in Part V' (see pp. 97–9). Here, then, is the continuation of the cults that Frazer had analysed, while, with the inclusion of the ghostly figure that appeared to an Antarctic expedition – 'I forget which, but I think one of Shackleton's' – there is conveyed to us the idea that throughout history mankind cannot recognize his resurrected saviour.

The next section portrays 'the present decay of eastern Europe', something which, as we have seen (see p. 14), concerned Eliot deeply. With the collapse of spiritual values, with moral and financial ruin after the First World War and, further, the massive rises in population, there was at this time widespread fear of revolution. The example had already been set by Russia, and what Eliot pictures here is a swarming, mindless anarchy reared on the 'endless plains' of eastern Europe, which, with their 'cracked earth' and 'flat horizon', exactly correspond to the Waste Land itself. In other words, out of spiritual desolation come the forces of communism that threaten to lay flat the traditions of a more cultured Europe. These traditions, if not still potent, are at least a reminder of what can and has been achieved – they are the 'fragments' to shore against ruin. But now they are joined both to Russell's view of collapsing urban life (ll. 372–5 and see p. 9) and to Hesse's analysis of contemporary spiritual malaise (see pp. 123–5).

Hesse, in his *Blick ins Chaos*, had diagnosed the exhaustion of the European soul and had been excited by its yearnings towards the mystical east with its promise of the creation of a new type of man: imaginative, potent and, above all, spiritual. He detected, in other words, the movement towards a revival such as Eliot also wanted, but he saw it emanating particularly from Russia and from what he analyses as 'Dostoeveskian man'. Eliot, on the other hand, while certainly welcoming a revival of the spiritual life, could not envisage it coming from Russia. Rightly, he saw Soviet communism as the triumph of a materialist philosophy which threatened all that he stood for to its very foundations.

The closing word of this section – 'Unreal' – returns us to earlier references to Baudelaire in 'The Burial of the Dead' and 'The Fire Sermon' (ll. 60 and 207). If the cities Eliot lists (ll. 374–5) are threatened with destruction by the 'hooded hordes', they are also suffering from an internal corruption. This, as we have seen, is reflected in the sterility of their sexual life, and the following section (ll. 377–84) returns us to the neurotic woman of 'A Game of Chess'. Her neurosis there (ll. 108–38) is now developed into a wholesale *Walpurgisnacht*, a nightmare of horror and destruction in which the entire world is seen collapsing into the waterless desolation of the Waste Land, a desolation whose spiritual failure is emphasized by the Biblical allusion in the last line (see pp. 132–3).

Eliot's Notes comment thus on 'What the Thunder said': 'In the first part of Part V three themes are employed: the journey to Emmaus, the approach to the Chapel Perilous (see Miss Weston's book) and the present decay of eastern Europe.' We have traced the first and third of these elements. The next section (ll. 385–94) now brings us to the Grail legends.

We should see the Grail legends in the wider context of what we have already been examining. The 'hooded hordes' of eastern Europe are massed on the outer, desolate edges of the physical and spiritual Waste Land, and they threaten it with destruction through the sheer power of their numbers (ll. 366–76). Old European culture is threatened by the collapse of spiritual and sexual certainty, and the result of this is a Waste Land given physical and metaphorical shape by the landscapes that Eliot has included throughout the poem. Many of these, as we have seen, derive from earlier works in which the equation of the moral and physical was made (see, for example, pp. 95, 99–100 and 132–3). In this, the last part of the poem, this landscape of ruin becomes a place of purgatory and quest for spiritual insight (ll. 331–94). It is, at one and the same time, a symbol of contemporary devastation and the period of spiritual inertia after the death of the god – be he Frazer's or the New Testament's (see pp. 134–5). It is also, and again simultaneously, the Waste Land through which the questing knight has to ride in his pursuit of spiritual truth embodied in the ceremonies of the Grail castle (see pp. 102–3). Eliot refers us at this point to *From Ritual to Romance*, since the argument of that book presents the medieval tales as the direct descendants of the cults analysed by Frazer (see pp. 99–101). In these works, of course, the quest is seen in fundamentally Christian terms, and so, by extension, Eliot can show a continuity of the death of the God and the search for redemption running unbroken from the Old Testament, the cults of Adonis and the Hanged God, through the very earliest days of Christianity, and on through the Middle Ages to the present. The questing knight is at one with all other seekers after truth.

But he finds that the chapel is empty (l. 398). There are no strange rites of initiation, no preparation for further revelations. Here is 'only the wind's home'. The seeker has pushed himself to the absolute and found nothing. The traditions are dead. It is at this moment that there comes the glimpse of partial salvation:

> Only a cock stood on the rooftree
> Co co rico co co rico
> In a flash of lightning. Then a damp gust
> Bringing rain

This clarion call announces a new stage symbolized by the possibility of rain, of the Waste Land redeemed. For the moment it is 'far distant'. But the thunder is no longer dry and sterile. The flash of lightning, the flash of spiritual as well as actual illumination (see p. 122), prepares us for the voice of God and his command to creatures to 'give, sympathize, control', to free themselves, in other words, from the world of selfish desire.

Giving is seen as the giving of self in love (ll. 401–9). It is the moment of surrender and the loss of selfhood, something beyond words and beyond recording (see ll. 405–9 and p. 83). It is the glimpse 'into the heart of light, the silence' which failed in 'The Burial of the Dead'. Nonetheless:

> By this, and this only, we have existed

Eliot here reaffirms human values, the possibility of a transcendent love beyond the neurosis of 'A Game of Chess'. But the revelation is wholly private and inexplicable to others (ll. 405–9).

Sympathy, the giving of oneself to many others in charity, is here defined by its opposite: treachery, imprisonment, darkness (ll. 411–16 and see pp. 115–16). Such behaviour brings guilt and the feeling of failure, but, as the quotation from Bradley in the Notes suggests, the world can only be experienced subjectively. Other minds are not fully knowable and each man is finally alone with his sensations, 'a circle closed on the outside', through which he cannot break. True sympathy is all but impossible.

The original passage of the *Brihadaranyaka Upanishad* suggests the third virtue is *self*-control, the restraint voluntarily placed on desire. Eliot's interpretation is somewhat different. He takes a moment of oneness while sailing and compares it to the wished-for unity of lover and beloved (ll. 418–22). Contented human passion is again the value most to be prized, but here control becomes not self-constraint but the feeling of order derived from a rightly conceived unity with one's beloved and the elements – the prosperous world of water and returned affection.

However, the moment of revelation and of possible potency is not complete and, as we shall see, is not final either. What the thunder urges on man is love, the free surrendering of self and the consequent spiritual and psychological health of the private and universal Waste Land redeemed. But such loss of self can be neither complete nor permanent. Mankind is obliged to return to his own closed circle of perception (see note to 1. 411). The best he can hope for is a remembered glimpse of what has been or could have been experienced, and the Narrator is forced to recall this in isolation.

It is with such isolation that we end (ll. 423–33). The 'arid plain' may be behind him, but the Narrator is still the Fisher King (1. 424), still the psychologically wounded man. No permanent salvation has been vouchsafed. The isolated figure asks desperately: 'Shall I at least set my lands in order?' Can he right his own Waste Land, if nothing else?

The answer (which is not direct) is given in the bewildering collage of quotations with which *The Waste Land* ends. The city in which the Narrator lives is still 'unreal', still 'falling down' (1. 426). There is no guarantee whatsoever of cultural continuance. And what of the unhappiness of love? The quotation from Dante's *Purgatorio* – the glimpse of Arnaut Daniel returning to the refining fire (1. 427) – intimates on the one hand that 'burning' and desire have not been conquered, but also suggests that perhaps the burning is not without purpose. Maybe it will lead to purgation, to acceptance one day into some higher order (see pp. 117–18). But the sterility of the Waste Land is still very marked. The reference to the *Pervigilium Veneris* (1. 428) and the myth of Philomel (see pp. 131 and 77–8) suggest first that in the failure of love the poet has been rendered mute. The failure of love is the failure of poetry and art. Love is still horribly close to neurosis and barbarism, and the result is collapse, personal and cultural. *The Waste Land* is, as the quotation from de Nerval beautifully suggests (1. 429), a place of cultural ruin, of the Aquitainian prince at the shattered tower. And it was the aristocracy of Aquitaine who had fostered the lyric poetry of the troubadours, the artistic potency which has now gone to waste (see pp. 117–18). The Narrator must pick his way across the wrecked landscape of his inheritance and search out the gleaming fragments of the past (see 1. 430). It is with these that he believes he can shore himself up 'against my ruins'. Or can he? They are not really enough, and, besides, as we have repeatedly seen, the literature of the past is not merely a comfort or a soft option. It contains barbarism, violence and horror, even the threat of insanity:

> Why then Ile fit you. Hieronymo's mad againe.

There remains only the partial glimpse, the divine instructions to give, sympathize and control (1. 432). Only in love and in the loss of selfhood – however brief they may be – can modern man, isolated among the ruins of his culture, threatened by enemies within and without, his myths broken and his emotions wrecked, glimpse for a moment the possibility of 'the Peace which passeth understanding'.

3. *The Waste Land*:
Varieties of Poetic Method

To express the immensely wide variety of responses in *The Waste Land*, Eliot developed an equally wide – and revolutionary – variety of poetic approaches and techniques. We shall examine these here. We shall begin with his description of the modern, concrete world and discuss the methods by which this is related to the timeless world of the poem through use of 'the mythical method' (see also pp. 26–30). This will require us both to analyse the rhetorical structure of the poem and to examine Eliot's discussion of the nature of time. Having then looked at the poet's conception of his place within the traditions with which he was working, we shall examine finally some of his images. Such matters – seemingly so diverse – are the tesserae of the poem, the individual units of which the whole mosaic is composed. A clear view of them, both of what they are in themselves and of their relationships, will enable us to appreciate the whole for the profound and moving poem that it is.

The physical world: from reportage to surrealism

> *Man passes through a forest of symbols.*
> Baudelaire

The Waste Land is a poem of great intellectual complexity, and a guide to it such as this is bound to stress its abstract nature. Nonetheless, when we read the work, we are aware of the acutely observed physical world that Eliot presents. *The Waste Land* is a poem full of colour, sound, voices and people doing things. Without this it would fail to involve us, and the wide range of Eliot's references would be an inert, inchoate mass. For purposes of analysis, we may look at the physical world of *The Waste Land* under a variety of headings. These are not separate, watertight compartments, but ways of elucidating the range of Eliot's descriptions and, in particular, the different degrees of symbolism that such descriptions contain.

Contemporary locations

First, there are those descriptions whose principal purpose is to root the poem in the contemporary physical world. Many of these are just names of places: the Hofgarten (a public park in Munich), localities in London such as King William Street and the church of St. Mary Woolnoth, the Cannon Street Hotel or 'a public bar in Lower Thames Street'. Incidental details are sometimes added to these: drinking coffee, for example, or the 'dead sound' on the ninth stroke of the church bell. Such details give – at least to parts of the poem – a local habitation and a name.

Symbolic impressionism

Similar to Eliot's use of specific place-names is his mentioning of such things as talk of demobilization, false teeth, 'hot gammon' and Mr. Eugenides's 'pocket full of currants'. These details are vivid and exact. They have something of a documentary's focus on real life. But, of course, they are chosen with a purpose, a purpose that becomes clearer if we examine the picture of the typist's bed-sit. This again is highly exact. We see her clearing her breakfast, lighting her stove and laying out tinned food. We see her divan that folds into a bed, her underwear, and, finally, we hear her record-player. Such details are not chosen at random. Precisely because they are so closely observed, they suggest emotions about the world in which they belong. They have been selected to convey the impression of a slight, tawdry, life-denying existence. As such, they help to prepare the reader for the typist's seduction by the clerk, for much of the sheer pointless vulgarity of that is suggested by the physical world in which it takes place. And it is precisely through this emotional effect of the scene – its depressing banality – that it both joins the wider discussion of sexual sterility in the poem and, at the same time, makes that discussion itself concern people in the modern world.

This ability to create a world of moral and emotional suggestion through physical facts shows the clear influence of Baudelaire on Eliot's work (see pp. 109–13). This is particularly emphasized by the fact that both poets were concerned to present the nature of the spiritual life in the modern city. Just as in *L'Ennui* Baudelaire recreates that mood by presenting the cat, the clock and the playing cards in his own rather sad apartment, so Eliot conveys at least part of his theme of spiritual blight through exact observation of the typist's bed-sit. The physical world of both poets encapsulates their emotional and moral one.

But Eliot had to go further than this. The scene we have just been describing – and others such as the pub gossip in the second half of 'A Game of Chess' – are examples of what we may call 'symbolic impressionism'. The physical details remain in the foreground, but are so selected and arranged that they give an impression of a world of emotional sadness and loss. The false teeth and tinned food symbolize a complex of emotional impressions, impressions of squalor, poverty, impotence, joylessness and so on. It was precisely these responses that Eliot wanted to analyse further. Merely to evoke them was not enough. He needed to ask what was wrong with the world that such life-denying matters were the dominant forms of the day.

Symbolic synchronicity

Such questioning led him inevitably to more abstract concerns: why had sexual and artistic potency failed, why is modern man's spiritual life so bankrupt? At least part of the answer involved an examination of the past, when such sterility was not the invariable rule. As we have seen, Eliot looked at the fertility cults of the ancient world, in which the sexual and spiritual life were joined in an affirmation of potency (see pp. 94–9). He looked at the Grail legends, where such matters were united to the Christian view of life (see pp. 99–103). He also examined the literature of the past – Dante and Shakespeare in particular (see pp. 113–15 and 137–40) – where a positive sense of love and joy could also be found.

To include such matters in his poem, to make them both complete and emotive, Eliot adopted a further technique in the presentation of the physical world: the re-creation of life about him in terms of the language and ideas of the past. The closing section of 'The Burial of the Dead' (ll. 60–68) is a good example of this.

What these lines present is a picture of commuters rushing into London. It is both exact and immediate. We are told the time of day, we see the crowds flowing across London Bridge, we hear their sighs, we see how they hold their faces. We learn where they are going. On the level of 'symbolic impressionism', we get the strongly felt sensation of rush, reluctance, stress and the depersonalized nature of the modern world of work. But we also get more. The two references to Dante in ll. 63 and 64 (see pp. 114–15) make us realize that while our immediate impressions are correct, Eliot wants us to relate these impressions to something more explicit – a richer analysis of spiritual decay than our own unaided sensations can provide. He wants us to see how such a world as he presents here is the moral and spiritual equivalent of Dante's Hell, that these commuters are so wretched because, like Dante's sinners, they have denied the spiritual life or are unable to find salvation.

Why not tell us this directly? Why bring in Dante? The reason is important and relates crucially to Eliot's method. Eliot wishes to show us the bankruptcy of the present. To be bankrupt is to lack the power to act on the world, and the modern world, being bankrupt, does not contain the wherewithal to analyse itself from its own intellectual resources. This was not true of the past. Dante's sinners suffer in one corner of a vast, coherent universe that includes love, beatitude and spiritual power. These have now been lost. What was once a small part of Dante's existence has here become the whole of ours. When we contrast our modern world – incoherent and blighted as it is – with the lost and far more comprehensive world of coherence and potency in Dante, then we glimpse ourselves more powerfully. We see our bankrupt state in a wider perspective. We come to see how the vividly observed, modern, physical world symbolizes spiritual death, and, when this is placed in the context of the past, the time when mankind knew not only spiritual bankruptcy but also the way beyond it, then we see how truly wasted our own age is.

We could perhaps call this technique of juxtaposition 'symbolic synchronicity'. Through it, we are made to see the modern physical world encapsulating the spiritual death that has been known in all periods. We see the past and the present working together in synchronization. This is a crucial part of Eliot's technique of analysis in the poem. Such blight as Eliot describes is, at one and the same time, both itself and the spiritual blight of all periods. The bitter irony lies in the fact that whereas in the past there were ways out of it, now there are not. The references to Dante, vegetation cults, Grail legends, Renaissance poetry and the rest provide a vocabulary for such spiritual decline and a comment on the broken and blinded modern world.

Symbolic landscapes

To a large extent, Eliot's poem is, naturally enough, a landscape poem. We have seen already how references to the modern city landscapes of London root it in an immediate physical world, a physical world that, nonetheless, symbolizes its spiritual deadness. There are, however, a number of landscapes in the poem – the Old Testament desert of ll. 19–30, the river banks of ll. 173–96, the mountainous world of ll. 331–394 and the Narrator's 'arid plain' at the close, for example – that are principally symbolic. Instead of the modern physical world being presented in such a way as to symbolize its bankruptcy, the passages referred to here are primarily symbolic and only secondarily realistic. We interpret them as emotional states presented as pictures. They exist more in our imagination than in the real world.

To appeal to the imagination they must, nonetheless, be vividly described. Let us look at the desert of ll. 19–30. The dominant impression here is of barrenness, brilliant light and drought. Here is a world of scrub plants and insects, sand and rock. We are made to feel its impotence and desiccation in our own selves. We are made to feel that we are there both physically and at the present time. But we are also made to feel that this desert has existed throughout the ages. The reference to Ezekiel (1. 20) confirms this. Our immediate impression of what the desert symbolizes is the same as what it has always symbolized: man alone, impotent and afraid without God. The desert is thus a further example of 'symbolic synchronicity'. However, because the desert is principally a state of mind and only secondarily a physical location, we can relate it to the other symbolic landscapes of the poem: the river banks of the second section of 'The Fire Sermon' and the more vivid mountainous world of 'What the Thunder said' (ll. 331–94).

Both the symbolic landscapes of 'The Fire Sermon' and 'What the Thunder said' are analogous to that in 'The Burial of the Dead' in their presentation of a desiccated horizon that we are meant to interpret as the physical equivalent of a psychological and spiritual state. All three are places of penance, fear and suffering. The landscape of 'the dull canal' in 'The Fire Sermon' relates particularly to that of the Waste Land of the Grail legends (see pp. 99–100), as does that of 'What the Thunder said' (ll. 385–90), which, in addition, contains references to the Old Testament (see pp. 132–3). Again, the sense of physical stress is marked. Finally, the mountainous landscape of 'What the Thunder said' is a place of agony and quest, of fear, violence and nightmare vision. In the opening lines, the God-figure (Jesus in this case) has been slain. The result is suffering and confusion in a terrifying landscape of hallucination, a time without a risen God (see pp. 95–6) and, subsequently, when the god has risen, of a time when he is not recognized (ll. 359–65). As in the second section of 'The Burial of the Dead', there is rock and sand here but no water. We then go on to see the actual physical destruction of the images of western culture (ll. 366–76). Similarly, in 'The Burial of the Dead', we are shown 'a heap of broken images' and then taken into the shadow of the rock to witness 'fear in a handful of dust'. In the last part of the poem we are taken into the Grail chapel (ll. 385–90 and see pp. 102–3), only to find that it is empty.

Surrealism

These landscapes are landscapes of the mind. They are the symbolic expression of the spiritually sterile. Eliot adds one further development to this that is particularly interesting: the mind at the end of its tether breaks down. Visions of insanity career across it with a dreadful energy (ll. 377–84). This is a world of hallucination, and such anarchic patterns from the disturbed unconscious were something that greatly interested

Eliot's contemporaries. Under the influence of Freud and psychoanalysis particularly (see pp. 10–11), artists in several media tried to convey this world of illogical unconscious power. The movement is known generally as surrealism, and Eliot made distinguished use of its visual world in *The Waste Land*.

The first example of the world being presented in surrealist terms comes in the opening lines of 'A Game of Chess'. Here, as Eliot describes the woman's over-luxurious boudoir, so it ceases to be something concrete (one might compare the typist's bed-sit) and develops instead into a hallucinatory expression of the Narrator's terror and the woman's own neurosis. At once highly physical, it goes beyond the bounds of the merely real. It is an expression of power and fear, and, with the description of the rape of Philomel (ll. 97–100), a comment on its own barbarity. The whole culminates in a brilliant surrealist image:

> Under the firelight, under the brush, her hair
> Spread out in fiery points
> Glowed into words, then would be savagely still.

A similar image leads into the second surrealist sequence (ll. 327–84), and both the contents of this passage and its methods are of the greatest interest.

The picture of the woman brushing her hair in 'A Game of Chess' helps to define the Narrator's fear of a feminine sexuality (see pp. 21–3 and 81–5). This is a particularly vivid aspect of the general discussion of neurosis in the poem. That neurosis, of course, is both a result of and a contribution to the breakdown of psychological and spiritual coherence, which is the subject matter of Eliot's poem. In the surrealist passage in 'What the Thunder said', these two are brought powerfully together. As in a dream (the basis of much surrealist imagery), so images of the physical world here combine with symbolic ones, with distortions and horrors that we must understand purely through our intuition (ll. 379–383). Finally, to relate this sexual neurosis to religious fear (and so combine the themes of his poem), Eliot uses the symbolically synchronous image from the Old Testament in the last line of this section. Surreal horror has been known in all generations.

Madame Sosostris

We have been discussing the relation of Eliot's physical world to his symbolic one. A further passage should be examined before we can analyse the closing lines of the poem. That passage is the consultation with Madame Sosostris. Eliot deftly places this, the most symbolic passage of the whole work, in the contemporary physical world by reference to the woman's cold and her concluding comments about needing to be 'so careful these days'. During the reading, the patterns of talk – and Eliot's ability with dialogue is one of the poem's great strengths – similarly convey an impression of the present-day world. Such immediacy, however, serves an entirely symbolic purpose. Though actually dealt on to the table in front of the querent, the Tarot cards provide a great deal of the symbolism of the vegetation rituals (and hence of western religion in general) on which the poem is structured (see pp. 104–7).

'The arid plain'

Much of what we have been discussing is brought to a climax in the last eleven lines of the poem. There is, first of all, a strong sense of physical location: 'upon the shore ... with the arid plain behind me'. But we realize, of course, that this landscape is at one with the other symbolic landscapes in the poem. It is both contemporary and synchronized with the Waste Lands of all time. Its physical nature is at once emotive and symbolic. Here, finally, is a landscape at once physical and metaphorical, contemporary but timeless, here yet everywhere. It is a landscape which is desolate and threatened, but which, in its physical, symbolic and surreal forms, defines exactly Eliot's Waste Land world.

The rhetorical structure of *The Waste Land*

> *Only when the form is quite clear to you will the spirit become clear to you.*
>
> *Robert Schumann*

The way in which *The Waste Land* is constructed is at one with Eliot's themes in the work. Form and content, subject and treatment, correspond. This is a matter which, while complex, is most important. Discussing the various issues it raises should help us to clarify the intellectual basis of the work and so give proper grounds for informed comment on Eliot's particular handling of his themes of sexual and spiritual decline. In this section we shall therefore re-examine his use of myth as a framework for ideas and comment; the relationship of this to the figure of Tiresias; Eliot's use of quotation and allusion; the way in which these reflect his conception of time and the true poet; the manner in which the sudden shifts and juxtapositions relate to the issue of 'free verse'; and, finally, the structural nature of Eliot's imagery.

The 'mythical method'

'It is only through magic that life stays awake.' The quotation is from the German poet Stefan George, but it points to the dilemma at the heart of *The Waste Land*: the sterile mediocrity of modern life now that it has cut itself adrift from the once potent and charismatic myths that sustained it. These myths, as we have seen, form a tradition of spiritual health; but before we analyse their chains of connection, one point about their use must be made clear: the myths are not intended to be the rigid, logical framework on which the poem is founded. They are not like the iron skeleton of a tower block, the 'real' structure which we can get down to once we have pulled away the surface accretions. If they were indeed the 'truth' we were trying to get at, then Eliot's poem would only be some sort of word-game, a more or less pretty distraction from our real task. And our task would be that of anthropologists collecting old tales rather than that of critics trying to make clear their experience of the poem. Eliot's allusions to myth and poetry are not the hard core of his poem. They are things that deepen and universalize it if we are alert to the feelings which they raise and if we can sense how these feelings relate to the present. It is in this way that we should experience Eliot, in his own definition of the mythical method, 'manipulating a continuous parallel between contemporaneity and antiquity'.

Let us first get some overall view of them. The myths that Eliot uses commence with the vegetation ceremonies of the ancient world in which the death of the divine but mortal lover of the fertility goddess imposed sterility on the world. Then, through a process of sympathetic magic, the believers took part in the redemption of both their deities and the spiritual blight on their lives (see pp. 94–9). The modern world cannot do so. It is locked in the time when the god is dead but has not been resurrected or, when he is, is not recognized. These traditions (as Eliot derived the argument from Frazer and Weston) were passed on to Christianity and found a particularly powerful means of expression in the medieval Grail myths and the imagery of the Tarot cards (see pp. 99–107). The magisterial comprehensiveness of Catholic theology as expounded in Dante provided a further coherent system of spiritual values (see pp. 113–18), while, from the troubadour love poets from whom Dante himself derived much, sprang the European traditions of love poetry which, particularly in seventeenth-century England, offered an analysis of romantic passion at once evocative, celebratory and socially enhancing (see pp.

117–18 and 135–40). The apotheosis of romantic passion in Wagner's *Tristan und Isolde* provided a further framework for analysis in the poem (see pp. 125–6).

However, Eliot's range of reference is not simply European. He had himself studied eastern religion, and at the close of 'The Fire Sermon' he unites this to western traditions through the 'collocation' of St. Augustine – a figure from the late classical world who had come to see asceticism as his way out of spiritual deadness (see pp. 127–9) – with the Buddha, who – after a similar appreciation of the value of denying the senses – had come to preach spiritual health through the avoidance of desire (see pp. 119–20). Buddhism itself is a refinement of the tenets of Hindu beliefs (see pp. 121–3) and, with the inclusion of the Lord of Creation incarnated as Indra, the God of Thunder, in the last section of *The Waste Land*, Eliot closes his circle by presenting a deity whose rules of conduct promise spiritual insight and the rain which may redeem at one and the same time the parched physical landscape of the Waste Land and the spiritual blight of the Narrator. This redemption is, however, by no means certain, and the concluding paragraph of the poem combines desperation and the longed-for potency of faith (see pp. 47–8).

So much for the positive remains of myth. We should look now at those areas of the spiritual traditions of the east and west that provided Eliot with a vocabulary of despair.

The vegetation myths themselves are crucial here. The mourning cries of the worshippers of Adonis offer a vivid picture of the Waste Land (see pp. 95–6). Here is a place of blight and panic, of life drained of vigour and potency. This is equally true of the devastated territory of the Fisher King (see pp. 99–101). Suffering from a seemingly incurable psychosexual wound and deprived of the redeeming mysteries of the Grail, he too languishes in sterile anguish. The Catholic theology of Dante again provided an anlysis of blight, for the inhabitants of the first divisions of the *Inferno* live in hopeless spiritual despair (see p. 115). In addition, the prophets of the Old Testament, exiled in the fruitless sands of the desert and aware of the wretchedness of life without redemption, offer further analyses of the Waste Land (see pp. 132–3). Finally, when Eliot turned to eastern religion, the sermons of the Buddha and the teaching of the *Upanishads* (see pp. 119–20 and 121–3) provided glimpses of sterile, burning lust and the need for redemption and rain.

Here is a vast web of traditional knowledge, knowledge of spiritual blight, sexual sterility and the myths and practices by which this condition may be overcome. It is these experiences which we are required to hold in our imaginations and memories. If we do so, then we shall have the necessary patterns of spiritual, emotional and cultural sensation against which to measure the fragments of modern life that Eliot shows us. His poem does not need a plot – the manipulation of a consecutive chain of events in such a way that, through the contrivance of meetings, the intentions and actions of characters, moments can be created in which issues are discussed and problems revealed such that they comment not just on the tale but on the world of the reader involved with the text. Eliot already had such patterns in the myths and poetic culture which the informed reader possesses as part of his intellectual and emotional equipment. Thus, saved from the need of 'telling a story', Eliot could get on with the more important literary business of showing the modern world for what it is, or what he considered it to be. When, in 'A Game of Chess', for example, he has his anguished modern man (a figure whom we have learned to associate with both Tiresias and the Fisher King) ruminate on drowning while himself in a room that is a nightmare parody of the European traditions of love, we ourselves, from our knowledge of the culture in which we live, provide the references and experience that help to make up and deepen our response to his mental and physical environment. At the same time, we see how, for this representative modern man, these once coherent traditions are potent no longer. The man is in anguish amid 'a heap of broken images', images that derive from the traditions of myth with which Eliot deepens his poem.

Such is the 'mythical method' for which Eliot praised Joyce (see also pp. 27–9). In brief, it allows for a continuous series of parallels to be drawn between the past and the present. Sometimes this involves the contrast between modern life in all its tawdry ghastliness and the banished world of cultural potency; at other times it involves a pointing out of the similarities between the sexual violence and spiritual decay known in the ancient world and repeated in the contemporary one. In both cases Eliot is, to repeat, 'manipulating a continuous parallel between contemporaneity and antiquity'.

Tiresias

Just as our cultural inheritance deepens the analysis of ideas in *The Waste Land*, so the figure of Tiresias holds the poem's many characters together in a revealing synthesis. Eliot tells us this himself:

> Tiresias, although a mere spectator and not indeed a 'character', is yet the most important personage in the poem, uniting all the rest. Just as the one-eyed merchant, seller of currants, melts into the Phoenician Sailor, and the latter is not wholly distinct from Ferdinand Prince of Naples, so all the women are one woman, and the two sexes meet in Tiresias. What Tiresias *sees*, in fact, is the substance of the poem.

The figure of Tiresias is thus a special example of Eliot's use of the 'mythical method', of his 'manipulating a continuous parallel between contemporaneity and antiquity'. We should now examine this in further detail.

Eliot discovered Tiresias in classical sources: Sophocles, Seneca and Ovid (see pp. 107–9). As we have seen, Eliot often uses Greek myth – the rape of Philomel and the story of Diana and Actaeon, for example – to suggest barbarian cruelty in matters of sex. Tiresias is a further example of this, as the passage from Ovid that Eliot cites in his Notes makes clear (see pp. 107–8). Tiresias has had the experience of living in both genders, while his blindness and gift of prophecy are a direct result of his interference in a debate between the father of the gods and his wife as to whether men or women derive more pleasure from sex. Here, indeed, is a cruel chain of events; but, with the appearance of Tiresias in the Waste Land of Oedipus's Thebes, he becomes further associated with sexual violence, sin and punishment.

Tiresias is presented in these plays as a man of great age, and Eliot elaborates this to suggest that Tiresias has existed across all time and space as both the epitome and the observer of mankind's suffering. Because he is also male and female – an 'old man with wrinkled female dugs' – he has an intuitive understanding of both genders. He can appreciate simultaneously the world of the Prophets; the lover in the Hofgarten; the querent at Madame Sosostris's; Stetson; the man in 'A Game of Chess'; the 'carbuncular' clerk in 'The Fire Sermon'; Phlebas and the questor in 'What the Thunder said'. Simultaneously he is at one with the women: Marie and the two failed prophetesses, the Cumaean Sybil and Madame Sosostris; the women in 'A Game of Chess'; and the typist in 'The Fire Sermon'. And he is the surreal, neurotic lady in 'What the Thunder said'. In so being, Tiresias epitomizes the experience of all men and all women – of mankind itself, in fact.

Tiresias epitomizes mankind's experience not just across gender but also across time. We have seen that the references in *The Waste Land* range from the religions of the earliest western civilizations through those of the east to the present day. The great age of Tiresias, who has lived through all this experience, thus makes him the epitome not just of the personal histories of contemporary men and women, but of all mankind across the ages. He is a mythical figure who, in his own person, deepens the diverse and suffering characters of the poem, in the same way as the patterns of cultural and spiritual tradition which Eliot presents deepen its intellectual themes. To quote F. O. Matthiessen:

In this way [Eliot] can at once suggest the extensive consciousness of the past that is inevitably possessed by any cultivated reader of today, and, more importantly, can greatly increase the implications of his line by this tacit revelation of the sameness (as well as the contrasts) between the life of the present and that of other ages.

By means of the two analogous rhetorical devices we have been discussing – the 'mythical method' and the character of Tiresias – Eliot takes us to the heart of a central theme of *The Waste Land* and, indeed, of all his work: the nature of time.

The Waste Land *and the nature of time*

We have seen that Eliot's use of the 'mythical method' allowed him to show the continuity of the experience of the Waste Land across history: the unredeemed modern world is at one with the desert of the Old Testament fathers, the blighted landscape of the vegetation myths and the devastated realms of the Fisher King. We have seen how the figure of Tiresias complements this by drawing characters of both genders and all ages into one ambiguous, suffering and thwarted prophet. Thirdly, we have seen how Eliot's use of allusion and quotation defines the modern world by placing it in the context of past verbal and spiritual traditions of east and west: the Buddha and the *Upanishads*, the Old Testament, St. Augustine, Dante, Renaissance literature and many more. All of these techniques are at once matters of rhetoric – of the verbal construction of the poem – and of Eliot's understanding of the history of the modern world. In his poem he does not choose to explain modern man's predicament simply as a result of contemporary factors. *The Waste Land* is not just a picture of life in the early 1920s, what it was like and how it came to be thus. Rather, the poem is a meditation on the long experience of spiritual life and this is expressed through the sense of tradition in which the modern world is at one with the past. The wide range of religious beliefs, poetic expression and human experience that Eliot evokes in his poem form a tradition of spiritual knowledge, a wealth from the past which can only be earned by the scholarship which then provides the emotional context crucial to understanding the present.

Eliot wrote of these matters thus:

Tradition ... cannot be inherited; if you want it you must obtain it by great labour. It involves, in the first place, the historical sense, which we may call nearly indispensable to anyone who would continue to be a poet beyond his twenty-fifth year; and the historical sense involves a perception, not only of the pastness of the past, but of its presence; the historical sense compels a man to write not merely with his own generation in his bones, but with a feeling that the whole of the literature of Europe from Homer and within it the whole of the literature of his own country has a simultaneous existence and composes a simultaneous order.

'All time is externally present' as Eliot wrote in *Burnt Norton*, and it is through such synchronicity that *The Waste Land* works. It is what the rhetorical structure which we have been examining so far is designed to serve. The poem does indeed suggest 'the pastness of the past', the great distance between ourselves and historical times; but it also suggests how this inheritance is still at work, offering both criticism and a means of expression, analogies and comparisons. The method is, again, that of 'manipulating a continuous parallel between contemporaneity and antiquity', which Eliot praised in Joyce. It is in this way that the 'presence' of the past is surely felt in the poem.

Since this is the case, we should go on to examine how this form of analysis was at one with Eliot's convictions about how the mature poet works. As we do so, the ideas of 'impersonality' (see p. 17), learning and tradition that are central to Eliot's view of his vocation will also be seen for what they meant to him.

Tradition and the Individual Talent

Tradition and the Individual Talent is the title of one of Eliot's first published essays. It is at once an analysis and a manifesto. It reads with all the excitement of a young man of genius discovering himself as he writes. The passage discussed in the previous section was taken from the essay, and we should examine now the way in which Eliot's concern with time and tradition shaped his view of the poet's function.

Let us remove one piece of modern sentimentality at the start: the belief that a poet cannot 'express' himself if he is too learned, that scholarship in some way clips his wings. Solid learning was a requirement of most poets until fairly recently. Chaucer, Spenser, Milton and Donne were men of encyclopedic knowledge. It did not inhibit their humanity, nor does it prevent them from moving the civilized reader. So, too, with Eliot, who makes the following trenchant comment on the poet's need for erudition:

It will ... be affirmed that much learning deadens or perverts poetic sensibility. While, however, we persist in believing that a poet ought to know as much as will not encroach upon his necessary receptivity and necessary laziness, it is not desirable to confine knowledge to whatever can be put in a useful shape for examinations, drawing-rooms, or the still more pretentious modes of publicity. Some can absorb knowledge, the more tardy must sweat for it. Shakespeare acquired more essential history from Plutarch than most men could from the whole British Museum. What is to be insisted upon is that the poet must develop or procure the consciousness of the past and that he should continue to develop this consciousness throughout his career.

Why? Eliot's answer amounts to a description of the mature poet, the person who, aware that the accumulated traditions of his culture are more valuable – richer, wiser and more effective – than his own unaided impressions, surrenders himself to them. In Eliot's phrase, he has them 'in his bones'. Eliot writes that the poet 'must be aware that the mind of Europe – the mind of his own country – [is] a mind which he learns in time to be much more important than his own private mind . . .' As a result, 'The progress of an artist is a continual self-sacrifice, a continual extinction of personality.' The true artist, in Eliot's view, does not make his ego the centre of his professional interest; rather, he surrenders to the living stream of tradition, the true, traditional vocabulary and syntax of thought, in order to enrich it and be enriched by it. He becomes the spokesman of his civilization rather than the mouthpiece of his self. So much is obvious in *The Waste Land.* Consequently, 'The more perfect the artist, the more completely separate in him will be the man who suffers and the mind which creates; the more perfectly will the mind digest and transmute the passions which are its material.'

The mind of the mature poet is, in Eliot's image, a catalyst: it transmutes experience into poetry without itself appearing in that poetry. But, without the poet's mind, the poetry itself could not be written. What counts is not the degree of the poet's personal suffering but 'the intensity of the artistic process'. The passion lies in the poet's artistry, not his life. Finally, because that artistry – its skill, craftsmanship and force – derives from tradition, from the voices of the past talking together, we come to what may at first sight seem Eliot's most paradoxical statement on the nature of the true poet:

> We shall often find that not only the best, but the most individual parts of his work may be those in which the dead poets, his ancestors, assert their immortality most vigorously.

The true poet, in other words, is he who most fully appreciates his forebears, has gone to them and, with much effort, absorbed their cumulative wisdom to such a degree that he is now at one with them and able to recast the world in their mould, even, sometimes, in their phrases. He has joined the dead to continue their life in his own, to absorb and thus extend and modify them. It is in this way, through his educated sensibility, that the poet can genuinely manipulate the 'continuous parallel between contemporaneity and antiquity', which is both the form of *The Waste Land* and its means of analysis.

'These fragments I have shored against my ruins'

Eliot's aim to work within tradition in this way is crucial to our understanding of the methods of *The Waste Land*. It is – obviously enough – the reason why we have to share his culture, to be familiar with his sources. These are not pedantic extras, a vulgar way of making the poem intellectually respectable or just downright difficult. They are part of the very voice of the poem itself, the full chorus of the eastern and western traditions working in parallel. It is they who speak to us, not the troubled bank clerk. Eliot, by his own theory, is, as we have seen, merely the catalyst, the invisible quantity who has effected a new arrangement of these voices without himself rising stridently above them. It is with this in mind that we should now look further at Eliot's use of quotation and allusion in the poem.

We shall concentrate here on the use that Eliot makes of other men's poetry. It should by now be clear that this use is not ornamental or a form of plagiarizing, but central to the techniques of the poem. We have already noticed how allusions to Dante in the closing section of 'The Burial of the Dead' make that passage at once deeper and something more than a description of a single moment of time (see pp. 51–2). They place spiritual collapse within a tradition of analysis. The same is true of references to the Old Testament, Wagner and the Renaissance. What we need to appreciate now is why such tradition is so pressing a concern in *The Waste Land*.

In our brief review of the contemporary intellectual background to Eliot's work (see pp. 9–16) we noted the failure of science, sociology, religion and politics to provide a consistent metaphysical view of modern life. We saw, rather, that the modern world has proliferated a diversity of often mutually hostile views of man while, simultaneously, providing abundant evidence of the irrational nature of his behaviour. Science, faith and action could all be seen as suspect, particularly in the light of the flares over the battlefields of the First World War. The resulting incoherence was truly frightening, and intelligent men were bound to ask where security lay. Where, with faith, order and love shattered, could security be found? This is the question posed by the Narrator in the concluding paragraphs of the poem. What can he do for himself?

> Shall I at least set my lands in order?

The answer to this question lies in the rich and, to many students, baffling confection of quotations that fills the next four lines (ll. 426–9). Here are references to nursery rhymes, Dante, anonymous Latin and nineteenth-century French poems. What sort of an answer is this, we may ask.

The Narrator himself tells us that these lines are the fragments he has shored against his ruins. They are the voices of his tradition, pledges of cultural achievement. Identifying himself with these will, at least to some degree, afford him the coherence he so desperately needs. It is through these, in the preceding parts of the poem, that he has already been able to assert not only 'the pastness of the past, but its presence'. He has indeed written with the feeling that 'the whole of the literature of Europe from Homer and within it the whole of the literature of his own country has a simultaneous existence and composes a simultaneous order'.

But there is an important qualification to add to this, one that is vital if we are to appreciate the depth of religious analysis in *The Waste Land.* To be sure, Eliot shows his Narrator at the end submerging himself in his tradition. This is a start. At least it helps to shore up his 'ruins' against total decay. But, in itself, tradition is not enough. *The Waste Land* does not present the aesthetics of writing poetry as the solution to man's modern and age-old problem of spiritual blight. There is no suggestion here of redemption through art. Indeed, in this world of 'broken images', the creation of art is highly problematic. The long schooling in tradition is a prop, something with which to 'shore up' the 'ruins', but not a means of rebuilding. Besides, tradition itself offers no ready safety to the individual talent. It, too, has squarely faced and recorded moments of decline, despair, ruin and madness (l. 431). If we follow the allusions in the last part of Eliot's poem through to their sources, then they are very far from offering a panacea. Much more than art and tradition is required before we know 'the Peace which passeth understanding'. Man needs the faith towards which Eliot was struggling.

Parataxis – *'a heap of broken images'*

The mass of quotations at the close of *The Waste Land*, its violent juxtapositions of desperate and broken elements, is known as 'parataxis'. This device is useful, for, like all Eliot's rhetorical devices, it points to the deeper issues of his poem. Form and content are, to repeat, at one.

A clue to this technique is given in 'The Burial of the Dead', where the prophet declares that modern man knows only 'a heap of broken images'. We could perhaps imagine these as being like some ancient but deserted desert town: a pile of remains now Greek, now Roman, here Byzantine Christian, there pagan. The pile is confusing, sad with the sadness of broken things. We guess that they were once coherent and lively, the connections between them known by the sometime inhabitants. Now they suggest only the decay of traditional patterns.

So it is in the deserts of *The Waste Land*. Again, just as the quotations in the concluding paragraph are piled up against each other without grammatical conjunctions, so the sudden changes of scene in the poem are juxtaposed without the obvious syntax of thought. In 'The Burial of the Dead' we move from pre-war Germany to the deserts, to Wagner's opera-house at Bayreuth and on to London. All of these places, like the broken remains in the desert, were once part of a coherent pattern of myth and culture which has now collapsed. We both sense and long for their sometime order, but, instead, we have to pick our difficult and often confusing way amid the ruins of culture. Such is the form of the poem: that of the broken remains of coherence violently and sometimes confusingly juxtaposed.

Free verse

Such a form of reportage was bound to have its effect on the verse form of *The Waste Land*. A simple and regular pattern – say, the iambic line or the heroic couplet – would, by its very suggestion of coherence, have been wholly inappropriate. Something apparently much looser had to be chosen, and the rhetorical structure of the free verse form again reflects the content of the poem.

Free verse is a tricky proposition. Bad free verse – the sort that sometimes finds its way from classrooms and quiet culs-de-sac into school and parish magazines – is usually bad because it is feeble. Whatever it has to say would disappear under the scrutiny of a disciplined ear and mind. As Eliot himself said: 'The so-called *vers libre* which is good is anything but "free"', and he clarified the statement by defining Pound's usage:

Pound's *vers libre* is such as is only possible for a poet who has worked tirelessly with rigid forms and different systems of rhetoric.

In other words, as with all mature poetry, proper free verse can be written only when the would-be writer is so steeped in tradition that his ear is refined to the full potential of his language.

Eliot himself had the most delicate perception of 'the naked thew and sinew' of English, and no line of *The Waste Land* gives the impression of being arbitrarily cut off and continued on the next. We may take the first seven as an example. It might seem perfectly possible here to end each line with a comma before the present participle – perfectly possible, that is, until we hear how the little hiatus before 'breeding', 'mixing', 'stirring', 'covering' and 'feeding' emphasizes each, stresses their connection, and this at the expense of 'Lilacs', 'Memory and desire', 'Dull roots' and so on. The pattern highlights the reluctant activity contained in the verbs at the expense of the nouns, all of them names of things that would far rather be forgotten. Such artistry is not freedom at all. It is discipline of the highest order.

Such sensitivity to stress and pitch allows Eliot the most remarkable range of voices in the poem. Notice first of all, however, that the dominant impression throughout is of real speech. The many personae of the Narrator are convincing precisely through the tones of voice. This is most obvious in the two parts of 'A Game of Chess', but, as we shall see, it is rather more subtly used in 'The Fire Sermon', where the 'free' verse form allows not only the characterization we have just discussed but also the inclusion of direct quotation and a special form of imitation.

We have characterized *The Waste Land* as a poem of many voices and discussed the place of tradition within it. Both are the result of an active engagement with the literature of the past. The direct quotations (ll. 176, 179 and 202, for example) act as triggers for this. Analogous but more subtle in effect are those quotations that have been subtly emended (ll. 196–8, for example) and conflate passages from English Renaissance verse and, further, a general allusion to Eliot's 'Sweeney' poems (see pp. 22–3 and 81–2) with the particular concerns of the Narrator. The effect is simultaneously of Andrew Marvell's Renaissance pageant of love and death, John Day's sensuous lines and suggestion of violent sexual myth from the *Parliament of Bees* (see Eliot's note to l. 197) and Sweeney, the modern, sensual man of Eliot's earlier work. Sweeney, taking the foreground, becomes at once death (but death no longer gloriously evoked), the beautiful youth Actaeon (which he surely isn't) and a suggestion of the violence of sex. The collapse into folk poetry (see Eliot's note to l. 199) suggests the impossibility of writing celebratory erotic verse under conditions such as these, while the violent juxtaposition of the line from Verlaine makes us shockingly aware of what we have lost: purity and potency redeemed in the chapel of the Holy Grail.

Imitation of verse form – as opposed to verse content – has a similar effect. It often suggests how the modern world has abused or cannot sustain the cultural potency of the past. The introduction of the typist in 'The Fire Sermon' is a particularly good example of this. The content is sordid but exactly observed. The form is such that through it we hear the distant voice of a quatrain structure based on the iambic pentameter line. (This is the form, for example, of Gray's *Elegy Written in a Country Churchyard*.) In its pure form it can be shapely, melancholy and relaxed. Here the effect is to juxtapose these qualities with modern nausea. Once again, the form is central to the content and effect of *The Waste Land*. Through it we hear and are homesick for a past and potent culture while being forced to examine in cloying detail the impotent modern world.

The structural pattern of imagery in *The Waste Land*

A further device by which Eliot binds together the fragmented material of *The Waste Land* is imagery. Just as in seventeenth-century poetic drama the images can sometimes suggest the play's development, so in *The Waste Land* – a work necessarily lacking a clear progression – repeated images seen in various ways suggest the angles from which the content is being examined. Appearing and reappearing, inverted, extended, parodied, they help to suggest the enclosed and suffering world of the poem. We shall look first at the images derived from the elements: earth, air, fire and water; then at those images derived from the natural world; and, finally, at images culled from city life and music.

The imagery of the four elements

We have seen that Eliot was deeply indebted to the Elizabethan and Jacobean dramatists, drawing from them many images for his discussion of sexuality (see pp. 23 and 135–8). As is well known, these dramatists frequently used a cosmology based on the four elements of earth, air, fire and water. An imbalance in the proportions of these led to sickness. It is interesting to note that Eliot's poem – itself an analysis of a sick universe – also employs these.

EARTH

It is obvious that images of earth should play a crucial role in *The Waste Land*. The poem shows us a time of infertility, the season when the redeeming powers have vanished. From the 'dead land' of the opening through to the 'arid plain' of the close, we are made to cross stretches of 'cracked earth' and the dryness of deserts and mountains. All are images of impotence: the impotence both of nature and of man.

Round these images gathers a web of cultural references, references to the vegetation myths of antiquity and the analogous legends of the blighted realm of the Fisher King (see pp. 94–103). Both of these make it clear that the sterility of the earth and its redemption are dependent on man. Both relate this process of decay and resurrection to the state of his sexual and spiritual well-being. Third – and most importantly – this complex of myths concerns the *successful* renewal of the land. Through their rituals the Waste Land did indeed become fertile once more.

In the case of the vegetation myths, this process requires some insight into the psychology of ritual. We have learned from Frazer that the ceremonies of Adonis, Attis, and Osiris were annual ones, that the pattern of the death of the divine but mortal lover of the earth goddess, of her retreat and of the couple's subsequent reuniting followed exactly the earth's pattern of death at winter and revived procreation in the spring. We have seen further that the revival of the cycle was dependent on man's imaginative participation in it, the familiar patterns of behaviour by which, every year, he mourned the death and imitated the resurrection of Adonis. These forms of ritual are the means of man's imaginative participation in the divine. We can still see this in the Church year today. The darkness of the church at Advent and the subsequent lighting of candles, for example, are a way of being at one with a world lacking a redeeming Christ, and then, as the candles burn more brightly, of feeling how Christ is indeed the Light of the World. Ritual is thus man's imitation of supernatural patterns and his means of participating in them.

For the entire cycle to be effective, the ritual participated in during the period without gods must be deeply felt. The darkness of the church must truly be sensed as blindness before the candles are lit. Panic at the collapse of fertility must therefore be deeply expressed. The lamentations preserved from the ancient world (see p. 95) show how this latter was anciently accomplished, while the ceremonies in the Grail chapel, the redemption celebrated by the children's voices singing in the choir, again suggest how rich the final sense of imaginative fulfilment was.

In *The Waste Land*, however, there is only the mounting panic of infertility, the horror of the lamenting women. There is no ritual completion, no process of sympathetic magic by which death may be overcome. Instead, like men without gods in all times, we have to traverse a dead terrain: deserts (whether those of the Old Testament, ll. 19–30, or their contemporary equivalents, ll. 300–302), the brown, windswept horrors of no man's land (ll. 173–6) or the purgatorial mountains of 'What the Thunder said'.

Throughout the poem these landscapes appear and reappear. They are at once physical and metaphorical (see pp. 52–3). They form a pattern of imagery which binds past and present together – or, in the by now familiar definition of the 'mythical method', help Eliot in his maintenance of 'a continuous parallel between contemporaneity and antiquity'. If we allow our intuitions to work on the drama of what the myths present – the horror of a world without gods and the consequent decay of spiritual and sexual joy – then we can feel through them at one and the same time both their immediate physical awfulness and their age-old suggestion of moral collapse. It is in this way that images of earth bind the poem together and are at one with its methods and themes.

AIR

Just as the earth is corrupted, so is the air. Over the city of commuters, the city where Mr. Eugenides tries to solicit the Narrator, the cities that, in 'What the Thunder said', are collapsing, hangs the 'brown fog'. Here is a physical and moral murkiness. It is the fog that pollutes Baudelaire's Paris and out of which appear his seven old men (see pp. 110–11), spectral premonitions of death and fear. It is the starless gloom of Dante's Hell. It suggests the blindness of man groping his way without spiritual guidance. In its obscurity he goes about his corrupted life of spiritual inertia and sexual futility.

In the deserts, too, the air is discomforting. Here is the place of almost unbearable brilliance:

> ... where the sun beats,
> And the dead tree gives no shelter ...

The only escape from this brilliance lies in the shadows of the rock, but all that can be found here is 'fear in a handful of dust'.

As we have seen, the first part of 'A Game of Chess' shows us the collapse of sexuality into neurosis and fear, the terrors encapsulated in the myth of Philomela. We are shown how the wealthy and educated in this time of emotional anarchy have sunk into a state of seemingly irremediable illness. Here, too, the air is fetid. The breeze that blows in from the window 'freshens' nothing. Instead, the candle flames grow longer and smokier, while the scents, once meant to attract and allure, are seen only as 'strange' and 'synthetic'. They are unnatural. Extending the parallel to the description of Cleopatra's barge in Shakespeare's play (see pp. 137–8), perfume no longer purifies and draws the populace towards a near-miracle of sexual attraction. Instead, it overwhelms the fresh and natural. It eddies around until the man nearly faints. There is no allurement here. Instead, the perfume

> ... troubled, confused
> And drowned the sense in odours ...

The candle smoke and the scent mix until the whole is a suffocating horror, the exact physical equivalent of the emotions in the scene.

In 'What the Thunder said' we reach the extremes of hallucinatory horror. The city cracks and bursts 'in the violet air'. Here again there is no natural colour; rather, the air is at one with the horrors it illuminates, for again it is in the 'violet light' that the intensified surreal vision of the woman from the first part of 'A Game of Chess' reappears, drawing her 'long black hair out tight' while the baby-faced bats beat their wings and invisible voices sing out the end of the world.

FIRE

Just as the images of earth and air contribute to the physical description of *The Waste Land* – and at the same time symbolize its sexual and spiritual decline – so the references to fire draw the poem together. In 'A Game of Chess' the fire that burns in the woman's boudoir is the first of the images of flame that relate to sex. We have seen that sex is shown here as corrupt and unnatural, and we have seen too that the whole passage is a vividly surreal description of this. It is particularly ironic that the swimming green and orange flames should reveal 'a carvèd dolphin' – the fish that by tradition rescues the drowning man – while above this is displayed 'the change of Philomel'. The whole neurotic tableau is lit by fire and candelight – images of burning and lust that will be developed in 'The Fire Sermon'. All that these flames reveal here are images of unnaturalness and the violent barbarity of sex.

The title of the third section of the poem is taken from a sermon of the Buddha in which fire is seen as a metaphor of desire (see pp. 119–20). Flames have become more than those in the boudoir of the neurotic lady. No longer is it simply a question of thwarted sexuality and its symbols seen in their lurid light. Fire now symbolizes man's whole nature when he is fettered to desire, to the patterns of his own emotions and needs. Fire represents here the suffering of the man who has not seen that truth lies beyond the dictates of his personal wants.

It is at this moment that Eliot joins his references to eastern and western religion in the 'collocation' of Buddha and St. Augustine. Just as the Buddha saw unenlightened man burning with desire, so St. Augustine burned in the sexual depravity of late classical Carthage (see pp. 127–9). He, too, had believed the way to happiness lay in the fulfilment of bodily needs, but had found that the experience of sexual love was a torment. Physical release was no release at all. The emotional must be joined to the divine. Throughout *The Waste Land*, of course, we have seen the debasement of both when they do not work in harmony and, with the merging of 'these two representatives of eastern and western asceticism', we see the Narrator moving towards a clearer realization that the solution to his despair must lie in some form of genuine religious insight.

But access to the divine is not automatic. The opening of 'What the Thunder said' shows us the arrest and trial of Christ, the anguish of prayer in Gethsemane and the soldiers coming to arrest Christ by night. The God is captured and slain. Such is man's iniquity. And, when He has risen, He is not recognized. But the moment of partial spiritual insight in *The Waste Land* is also heralded by fire: the flash of lightning that precedes the teaching of the god of thunder. Lightning, as we have seen, is an eastern symbol of the moment of illumination (see p. 122). Here too it is not only the event that prefigures the advice from the *Upanishads*, but it is also the symbol that leads us on to the promise of Eliot's last and most complex image drawn from the elements – water.

WATER

Water is the most pervasive and subtle of Eliot's natural images in *The Waste Land*. Throughout the poem it is the thing most longed for. It is rain that will fructify the 'cracked earth' and extinguish the fires of sterile passion. It is a storm that will clear the fetid air. As with the other imagery of the elements, water is a part both of the physical world of the poem and of its metaphorical patterns of sexual and spiritual analysis.

We have seen that *The Waste Land* contains glimpses of positive vision. In particular, there is the moment in the hyacinth garden – the moment of love and loss of self – and the suggestion of a possible unity of lover, beloved and the elements that illuminates the third command – *Damyata* – of 'What the Thunder said'. Both moments involve water.

When we come to the scene in the hyacinth garden (ll. 31–42), we have already learned to associate gardens with rain. In the opening section we were told how summer 'surprised' the Narrator as it came with a shower across the Starnbergersee – a lake near Munich – and how, after taking shelter, he and his companion went into the Hofgarten. Now, in the hyacinth garden – which perhaps provokes thoughts of the same locale – we are shown a moment of potency and love. Here is a time of growth and loveliness, a moment of flowers, plenitude and 'wet' hair. It is framed by two snatches of Wagner (see pp. 125–6). The first, the opening words of *Tristan und Isolde*, suggest homecoming and home-sickness, a young and ardent longing. But already, in a tented cabin below, Isolde is sullen and resentful about her forthcoming marriage. She is crossing the waters to a hated land. She and Tristan have not yet drunk the love potion that will raise them to the full tragic grandeur of erotic passion, a torrent of music and poetry sustained throughout by images of the sea. Yet theirs will be a passion that can end only in death. The second quotation refers to this. We recall Tristan dying in his Waste Land castle, severed, it seems, from redeeming love, and able only to stare out at a desolate and empty sea.

In ll. 418–22 we are shown another moment of love and water. The Narrator is pictured sailing. He and the boat are at one with the sea. It is a moment of joy and control, a moment of unity that he would like to compare to his relationship with his companion. But, as we have seen, just as the moment in the hyacinth garden is doomed, fragmentary, so here the comparison is made in the conditional voice. Neither set of lines provides redemption. Both, however, in their expression of love and water, suggest the all but impossible way beyond the parched earth of the Waste Land.

It is through water that the physical Waste Land will be redeemed and, by extension, man be returned some promise of contentment. It is partly through this longing for rain that the images of earth are made effective. We have seen already how successful is Eliot's presentation of the desert in 'The Burial of the Dead', the place of sand, rock and brilliant light which is, consequently, the place of fear and spiritual blindness. We have seen, too, how this is analogous in its metaphorical content to the mountains of 'What the Thunder said'. In this latter section, indeed, the absence of water is heavily stressed. The Narrator pants in his thirst. Here there is only 'rock without water'. He can neither drink nor think, while, to heighten the drama, the air is riven with 'dry sterile thunder without rain'. In ll. 346–58 the mind rises to a tattoo of hysteria while the hermit-thrush, adding its notes to the bird song that forms another sequence of imagery in the poem (see pp. 77–8), mimics the dropping of water in a torturing parody.

But the pervasive water imagery in *The Waste Land* does far more than point the contrast between sterility and would-be redemption. Its place in Eliot's pictures of city life is particularly interesting. We have seen, for example, how, in Munich, summer came in a shower of rain across the Starnbergersee. The hyacinth garden – which we may well associate with the Hofgarten – blossomed and was a place of love and vision. In the neurotic world of the first part of 'A Game of Chess', however, rain is to be avoided. Claustrophobia is a dominant feeling here. The room is stifling and enclosed. As its trapped occupants think of ways of escape, one idea is:

> . . . if it rains, a closed car at four.

Here is another form of enclosure and sterile routine. The lovers will escape from the room only to the more confined space of a car in which they will be protected from the rain. The sterility underlying their relationship is heightened in this way. Not for them are the hyacinths and wet hair of the first section. These two can only sit in their car, staring out hopelessly at the unheeded symbol of fulfilment.

The Thames, too, plays a crucial role in Eliot's use of water imagery. We are introduced to it in the last section of 'The Burial of the Dead'. We are shown London Bridge (later to reappear 'falling down') and the crowd that 'flowed' over it. Here is a dry stream of spiritually dead humanity who will reappear in 'The Fire Sermon' when the Thames has been assimilated into the dried-out rivers of the eternal Waste Land. No longer is it the place of joy and potency that it once was, the place where Spenser's nymphs played innocently before the happy celebration of a marriage. 'The nymphs are departed'. Not a trace of them or their modern secretary equivalents is left – no litter, cigarette ends or 'other testimony of summer nights' (contraceptives?). Here is a place of death and desertion. The lone Narrator 'melts' into the figure of the ancient Hebrew prophets lamenting by the waters of Babylon. 'Jerusalem is fallen, is fallen.' And the river banks become (ll. 187–90) the desert lands of the Fisher King.

In the lovely section of ll. 266–306, Eliot's technique of 'manipulating a continuous parallel between contemporaneity and antiquity' is particularly effective. Expressed through the form of the Rhinemaidens' song from the last act of Wagner's *Twilight of the Gods* (see p. 26) – and hence suggesting the corruption and death of the old order – the Thames is seen in succession as a commercial thoroughfare (with memories here, perhaps, of Mr. Eugenides) and of the river pageant of Leicester and Elizabeth I (see Eliot's note to l. 279). The latter scene is particularly interesting, for, though it reminds us of the Enobarbus speech parodied at the opening of 'A Game of Chess' (see pp. 137–8) and is also contemporary with Spenser's nymphs, the pageantry here is not the glorious celebration of sex it might seem, but a hollow charade, a feckless abuse which suggests the trivialization of love even in periods of great cultural achievement. Allied to the image of water though they are, Elizabeth and Leicester are little better than the secretaries and their young boyfriends, 'the loitering heirs of City directors'. Finally, we return to the sterile modern period, the total collapse of an affair and the Narrator left on the sands at Margate. No longer is the Thames the great highway of merchants bringing the life-enhancing knowledge of their cults, no longer is it the place of culture and celebration. The debasement of love that it has always known (Elizabeth and Leicester, the modern 'nymphs') has taken it over as it runs out into the dry sands of Margate, the sands of the eternal desert.

Something of the past glory of London nonetheless remains and, with it, a suggestion of its sometimes spiritual health. We see this in ll. 257–65, which are some of the loveliest in the poem. The seduction of the typist has just taken place. We have been forced to witness the sordid, the trivial and the sad. In her post-coital lassitude, the girl, left alone, plays a record, which is heard by Tiresias. The music creeps by him 'upon the waters', as Ariel's music came to Prince Ferdinand (see pp. 138–40). The tune drifts 'along the Strand, up Queen Victoria Street', to be lost, perhaps, in the rush of City life. Yet, beneath the mindless clamour, music can still sometimes be heard, reviving happier memories of love. And with the thought of happy love comes the first suggestion of a more fulfilled life. We move down into Billingsgate, 'where fishmen lounge at noon'. Modern life is not to be seen exclusively in terms of 'fishing in the dull canal'. Here, in this area of London, there are at least the remains of a better life. There is the suggestion of a sometime potency and the glorious affirmation of religious strength in the church of Magnus Martyr, whose walls contain:

> Inexplicable splendour of Ionian white and gold.

This lovely line, perhaps more than any other in the poem, suggests what has now been all but lost, lost in the city of moral blight that has been Eliot's particular concern. How much is the beauty of Magnus Martyr still a force, how much is it just a reminder of what has been denied, its presence now little more than a piece of romantic archaeology? The London we have been made far more familiar with is the one where Mr. Eugenides tries to solicit the Narrator. It is the place where the myths of revival were once brought by the Phoenicians but are now, it seems, inexorably soiled. London is also the place where the ceremonies of the Grail chapel are horribly parodied. Instead of the ritual washing of feet – a reminder of the Last Supper – which preceded the mystical appearance of the Grail and the accompanying voices of children singing in the choir, we have only the brothel world of Mrs. Porter and her girls washing their feet in soda water. The grossly physical has triumphed. Sex is no means of insight. It has become a way of earning cash.

Water washes the sweat from the feet of a few tired tarts. In 'A Game of Chess', as we saw, it is something to avoid, while, in the consultation with Madame Sosostris, 'death by water' is something to fear. This is perhaps the poem's strongest denial of spiritual life.

The consultation with Madame Sosostris shows how blinded modern man has become. Despite her being:

> the wisest woman in Europe,
> With a wicked pack of cards

Madame Sosostris fails to appreciate the significance of the symbols she deals before the querent. Once – so Eliot learned from Jessie L. Weston – the Tarot cards had foretold the rising of the waters that would have flooded and revived the Waste Land (see p. 104). Now such relief is to be shunned. Its nature is misunderstood. The querent has come to try to win some form of spiritual insight for himself. It says much of the modern world that insight is looked for in such a way. But it is not found. The first card dealt (which traditionally revealed the current spiritual state of the querent) is 'the drowned Phoenician Sailor'. This is not a traditional member of the Tarot pack, and its symbolism clearly relates to the fourth section of the poem: the poignant and lyrical description of a drowning. The body of Phlebas the Phoenician sinks beneath the waves – the analogy to the ritual drowning of the vegetation god (see pp. 95–6) is clear – but this drowning does not lead to resurrection. Eliot's lines are an epitaph. As Phlebas sinks, so, in accordance with the old superstition about drowning, his past life floats in front of him. He passes 'the stages of his age and youth' and enters the whirlpool. The sea picks at his bones. He is not, like the supposedly drowned characters of *The Tempest*, transformed into something 'rich and strange'. He merely dies a mortal's death. As he does so, figures as diverse as Prince Ferdinand and Mr. Eugenides melt into him. Here is the quiet extinguishing of mortal life. There is no resurrection, only memory:

> Gentile or Jew
> O you who turn the wheel and look to windward,
> Consider Phlebas, who was once handsome and tall as you.

This is a lovely, melancholy moment, imbued with a sense of pathos and loss. Human experience sinks beneath the waves and nothing will revive or transform it. No resurrection follows. The Waste Land is not redeemed. There is only the welcome, cool, slow sinking into oblivion.

Those left alive must search out their own salvation. The Narrator melts into the figure of the questing knight tracking through the nightmare mountains of 'What the Thunder said'. He must go through a landscape of desiccation where 'sweat is dry and feet are in the sand', and, when he has come so far, he will find the Chapel empty. Only then, at the extreme point, will he feel:

> A damp gust
> Bringing rain.

In the far distance the black rain clouds have gathered, the jungle crouches and the thunder rolls. It booms out its rules of life: Give, sympathize, control. This is a command to moral action, not an immediate assurance of rain and redemption. At the close, the Narrator may have 'the arid plain' behind him, but he is still searching among his ruins. He is a long way from the hyacinth garden, 'the heart of light, the silence'.

The imagery of the four elements – earth, air, fire and water – the elements that from ancient times to the seventeenth century provided man with the physics of his universe, thus play a crucial part in this twentieth-century poet's description of his metaphysical universe.

75

Because his sexual and spiritual lives are out of joint, the elements, too, are unbalanced. In terms of the ancient cosmology, the world is sick: water does not fructify the earth, the air is corrupt and destructive fires rage within. The figure of God, who proverbially held these forces in check, is dead. Man is left very largely to his own resources.

Images from the natural world

Eliot also uses imagery from the natural world in *The Waste Land*. This is drawn mainly from three areas: flowers, fish and birds.

FLOWERS

It is with flowers that the poem opens. April breeds lilacs 'out of the dead land'. The process is painful and reluctant, for the Narrator's spiritual and emotional life has become identified with the inert winter soil, the 'forgetful snow' and the meagre existence of 'dried tubers'. Around the lilacs cohere the threads of memory, memories of life and of love. The flowers are, perhaps, analogous to those that decked the corpse of the god in the vegetation ceremony prior to his resurrection (see p. 96). Such forces of rejuvenation are unwanted here. Life means consciousness and pain. It is something to avoid, as Stetson does, in the unthinking rush of modern urban wage-earning. And it is with just these images of rebirth – both natural and, in their metaphorical context, relating to the vegetation myths – that the Narrator challenges him in the last part of 'The Burial of the Dead';

> 'That corpse you planted last year in your garden,
> 'Has it begun to sprout? Will it bloom this year?
> 'Or has the sudden frost disturbed its bed?

It is flowers, of course, that provide the imagery of love in the second section of 'The Burial of the Dead'. The moment in the hyacinth garden – the moment of potency and insight – is associated with an abundance of flowers which grow out of land revived and potent. Now that such values of love have been lost, we are left only with the desiccated plants of the desert (ll. 19–20) or, in the first part of 'A Game of Chess', the characteristic artificiality of:

> the glass
> Held up by standards wrought with fruited vines.

FISH

Comparable to this unnatural representation of the real world is the 'carvèd dolphin' on the mantelpiece in the woman's boudoir. Fish, as we know (see p. 100), are ancient symbols of fertility, but here they are only an ironic reminder of potency amid the stifling artificiality of decoration. And, of course, they relate to the imagery of the Fisher King of the Grail legends (see pp. 100–101). The Fisher King is the wounded ruler of a desiccated land. We were first introduced to him in Madame Sosostris's Tarot reading, where he is associated 'quite arbitrarily' with 'the man with three staves'. Gradually he emerges as a major image. In the second section of 'The Fire Sermon' the Narrator, 'fishing in the dull canal', becomes absorbed into him and we begin to see the whole landscape of the poem in terms of his wrecked kingdom. In 'What the Thunder said' we see the Grail knight, the questor who will cure him, riding through his realm, while, in the last paragraph of the poem, the Narrator, still searching for some form of coherence, is shown 'fishing' yet again.

BIRDS

Birds – and, in particular, their song – provide a third series of images from the natural world. They are associated with both the poem's main concerns: sexuality and the spiritual life.

As we have seen, Eliot often uses fragments of Greek myth to suggest the timeless barbarity underlying life. Nowhere is this clearer than in 'A Game of Chess' where the revolting story of 'the change of Philomel' (see p. 131) is the subject of the *trompe-l'œil* painting in the boudoir. (It is worth noticing that this particularly artificial form of painting, the deliberately heightened deception of space, is appropriate to the generally artificial atmosphere of the room.) The metamorphosis of Philomel is a particularly interesting story, since it suggests the relation between the violence of sexual desire on the one hand and its transformation into art on the other. At the moment of greatest danger to her, Philomel was metamorphosed into a nightingale, the bird of love whose song fills 'all the desert with inviolable voice'. It did so, too, for the Elizabethan John Lyly:

> What bird so sings yet so dos wayle?
> O 'tis the ravished Nightingale.
> Jug, jug, jug, jug, tereu, she cryes,
> And still her woes at midnight rise.
> Brave prick song! . . .

But just as 'Jug, jug' is slang for sexual intercourse, so Lyly's pun on 'prick song' (the descant version of a tune) suggests the brute physical facts that underlie the story. In *The Waste Land* the poetry has been forgotten. It has been replaced by snatches of cheap ballad (ll. 199–201) which grossly parody the ceremonies of the Grail chapel (see pp. 100–101) and suggest that purely physical sex and its accompanying violence are all that the modern world knows:

> Twit twit twit
> Jug jug jug jug jug jug
> So rudely forc'd.

Birds return in 'What the Thunder said'. Having helped to suggest the collapse of sex into barbarity, the hermit-thrush of ll. 356–7 mimics horribly the sound of dripping water in the hellish mountains, torturing the questor with an awareness of the actual and metaphorical desiccation around him. Finally, in l. 428 the swallow appears as a reference to the Philomela story and a reminder of the cruelty of sex and, in the quotation from the *Pervigilium Veneris* (see pp. 130–31), as the expression of an ancient, melancholy longing for freedom and the return of poetry, potency and inspiration.

Images of the city

Natural images provide much of the structure of *The Waste Land*, but we have seen too that it is a poem greatly concerned with city life. Edmund Wilson writes about this with his usual perceptive elegance:

> The terrible dreariness of the great modern cities is the atmosphere in which *The Waste Land* takes place – amidst this dreariness, brief images emerge, brief pure moments of feeling are distilled; but all about us we are aware of nameless millions performing barren office routines, wearing down their souls in interminable labours of which the products never bring them profit – people whose pleasures are so sordid and so feeble that they seem almost sadder than their pains. And this Waste Land has another aspect: it is a place not merely of desolation, but of anarchy and doubt.

This is a just characterization of the crowd flowing over London Bridge, the episode of the typist and the house agent's clerk, the place where Madame Sosostris touts for trade and where the lovers of 'A Game of Chess' indulge in self-destruction. In the absence of joyful sex and a co-herence of the spirit, the city in particular can highlight the awfulness of modern man's situation. The city is monolithic, depressing and sterile, a place of luxury and despair.

The presentation of the city relates in crucial ways to Eliot's use of the 'mythical method'. In its varying aspects it, too, shows the poet 'manipulating a continuous parallel between contemporaneity and antiquity'. For example, we should notice that while the modern city is at one with ancient places of moral ruin such as Jerusalem and

Carthage, the city has also been a place of potency, of Spenser, Wren, the *Prothalamium* and the church of Magnus Martyr. It is this multiplicity of aspects that we should hold in mind if we are to appreciate the depth and range of Eliot's analysis.

We have seen why and in what ways Eliot's picture of modern London is vividly physical (see pp. 49–51). We have seen how it presents the grinding world of modern work and sexuality. We have seen it compared both to Baudelaire's Paris and to Dante's Hell. As such, it becomes the paradigm of all cities, while its inhabitants, absorbed into the persona of Tiresias, again become part of Eliot's 'mythical method'.

In terms of the imagery of the elements, the city is particularly associated with water through the Thames. The river becomes a way of presenting both the city's glory and its decline. Once the port for the Phoenicians bringing knowledge of their life-assuring cult, it is now the desperate, fog-bound inferno where Mr. Eugenides solicits the Narrator, while, in 'The Fire Sermon', the leaves that 'clutch and sink into the wet bank' associate it with the devastated lands of the Fisher King. The glory of its churches may remind us of ancient images of fertility, but, finally, the sexual and spiritual emasculation of its inhabitants, their suffering and lusts, make it the model for all cities in times of collapse.

Such collapse is the cause of profound pessimism and even panic. Largely bankrupt though they are, the cities nonetheless contain much of the experience, the 'fragments' that the Narrator needs to shore up against his total collapse. This is made clear in 'What the Thunder said'. In ll. 366–76 we see a Waste Land at once physical and metaphorical that threatens the entire western world. On the 'cracked earth' of the 'endless plains', the forces of barbarism are gathering strength for their attack and, in the nightmare landscape of the mountains, the Narrator has a vision of the end of the culture he has known:

> What is the city over the mountains
> Cracks and reforms and bursts in the violet air
> Falling towers
> Jerusalem Athens Alexandria
> Vienna London

All of these great centres of western culture are now, like Baudelaire's Paris, 'unreal'. This is indeed an apocalypse. The broken Narrator is forced to sit among the ruins. The Aquitanian tower – the symbol of the refined culture of love poetry – is shattered. The crowds may once have flowed across London Bridge, but now it is 'falling down falling down falling down'. It is thus that *The Waste Land* ends – with the Narrator sitting amid the wreck of urban culture, threatened by madness and longing for the peace of the god. The cities are wrecked, but there is for him no clear vision of a new Jerusalem.

Images suggested by music

Musical images in *The Waste Land* range from the torrential passion of Wagner's *Tristan und Isolde* to children's nursery rhymes, from Ariel's song in *The Tempest* to Australian street ballads. This alone suggests something of the range of reference, the inclusiveness of Eliot's poem.

We have seen that the images taken from Wagner relate to water (see pp. 125–6). The two quotations that frame the moment of vision in the second section of 'The Burial of the Dead' both refer to the sea, while the song of the Rhinemaidens from *The Twilight of the Gods* joins the Thames to Wagner's deeply poetic, primordial river. The *Ring* cycle opens with the sustained E flat that represents the Rhine, while at the close of the work the river rises to flood the land in which humans and gods have acted out their tragedy. The analogies to the symbolism of *The Waste Land* are clear.

The music from *The Tempest* likewise relates to water – to images of drowning, metamorphosis and resurrection. Just as the character of Ferdinand stalks through the poem, so he is followed by Ariel's music 'invisible'. To Tiresias, observing the typist and the house agent's clerk, the music from the woman's gramophone becomes associated with Ariel's song. For the other woman of the poem, the hysterical lady in 'A Game of Chess', such sounds become debased into the distractions of

> O O O O that Shakespeherian Rag –
> It's so elegant
> So intelligent.

Great music thus plays a crucial role in *The Waste Land*. It suggests references to a higher culture and to many of the themes of the poem. Its melodies, now distorted, now themselves, help to bind the poem together. But if Eliot was aware of how great music could further his effects, he knew also how more popular modes could help. The snatch of Australian ballad in ll. 199–201, for example (I am given to understand that the full version of the original is highly bawdy), serves to make a grotesque parody of the ceremonies of the Grail castle (see p. 74). Finally, the nursery rhyme quoted in l. 426 suggests very aptly the collapse of urban culture.

4. Sexuality and Religion in *The Waste Land*

Sexuality

> *A man's attitude in sexual things has the force of a model to which the rest of his reactions tend to conform.*
>
> Sigmund Freud

Sexual insecurity, a belief that women are feckless or threatening and that intercourse degrades both partners, is a strongly marked theme in many of Eliot's early works. The title of the prose-poem *Hysteria* is significant, while the opening of *Dans le Restaurant* (the latter part of which, when translated, became 'Death by Water') suggests nothing so much as a remembered childhood trauma. Here, a 7-year-old boy, flirting with a younger girl, feels a moment of power and delirium which is destroyed as a fierce dog comes romping up to them. From such events, the psychoanalysts would say, is future misery made.

The Sweeney poems present a brothel world, physically nauseating and emotionally barren. In such works as *Sweeney Erect*, we see Eliot experimenting with contrasts between the sordidly modern and the evocative but violent culture of Greek myth. There are clear analogies here to the use he makes of the Philomel tale in *The Waste Land*. *Sweeney Agonistes: Fragments of an Aristophanic Melodrama* takes us to the core of this world, a world of kept common women, superstition and 'gentleman callers'. Sweeney is here the tragic anti-hero, hopelessly bound to a trivial inferno, a drinker and a womanizer who attempts to rise to some form of self-expression but, as he does so, can picture his world only where 'Death is life and life is death'. On the surface are boredom, fear and superstition, and underneath, as Sweeney says, are:

> Nothing at all but three things
> DORIS: What things?
> SWEENEY: Birth, and copulation and death.
> That's all, that's all, that's all, that's all,
> Birth, and copulation and death.
> DORIS: I'd be bored.

This is a shadow world, a moral slum. Superstition has taken the place of religion (the women read playing cards in a clear analogy to the Tarot scene in 'The Burial of the Dead'), sex is devalued and self-expression – let alone poetry – is all but impossible. Indeed, the only poetry that there is here is a parody of contemporary review numbers, a parody that sheers off into despair and talk of sex crimes. Perhaps the jazz choruses which the characters sing are like the tunes which the typist plays when the clerk has left her.

The world in which the typist lives is comparable to Sweeney's. We should perhaps imagine her as part of the crowd flowing over London Bridge in the first section of the poem. She is a fragment of the anonymous urban world of work, a world of routine and poverty, of bed-sit living and dispiriting sex. She does not even have a name. She does not rise to this level of individuality, and Eliot compounds such sadness by the way in which he presents her physical world. It is slatternly, frail and humiliating. It makes us feel bogged down in a world of objects that can only depress the spirit. There is no sense of the joyous here and no love. Sex is merely a routine.

As with the typist, so with her man. He, too, has no name. He is defined by what he does, and his being a 'small house agent's clerk' (notice the adjective) is designed to suggest a lack of educated feeling or responses and, perhaps, a certain lubricious cunning. He is an acne-ridden, cocky little womanizer. Far from stirring any excitement in his girlfriend, she remains 'bored and tired' in his company. With her resistance low and her spirits drooping, she is indifferent to his heavy-handed foreplay. He, more easily roused, commits his routine fornication. It is easy, unanswered, joyless. Sex has become as mechanical and dull as the world of work. Convention and the need for release dictate that it should take place, but there is no insight gained or life enhanced. The spirit remains in the dark, the dark of the landing outside the room.

And, as we have seen, Eliot makes the absence of redeeming joy more marked by the verse form he uses (see p. 66). Far from celebration, from the sheer rapture of the discovery of love, these people are, like Sweeney, faceless fragments, the living dead. As such, they merge in Tiresias's mind with the emotionally sterile across all time:

> (And I Tiresias have foresuffered all
> Enacted on this same divan or bed;
> I who have sat by Thebes below the wall
> And walked among the lowest of the dead.)

It is entirely appropriate that Tiresias should emerge at this moment, the half-way point of the poem. Just as the realistic physical world of *The Waste Land* alternates with symbolic or surreal landscapes (see pp. 52–4), so here we have a moment of the completely physical juxtaposed with a character who is himself a surreal figure from myth. Tiresias is, as we have said, the androgynous blinded seer who is the residue of all mankind's despair (see pp. 29–30 and 58–60). He is not, it should be noted, a homosexual figure. He is a hermaphrodite, both a man and a woman. Like the unconscious revealed by Freud, he is sexually ambiguous and, in theory, capable of any and all emotional and physical responses. However, far from being, like the unconscious, a well-spring of energies both acceptable and perverse, Tiresias is an exhausted figure. There is about him a feeling of utter deadness, of an infinite world-weariness. Again, like the neurotic analysed by Freud, he can only repeat experience again and again, and the experience he repeats is not one of joy and fulfilment, but a desolate and life-denying routine of sex. This he repeats both in his intuitive unity with the typist and the clerk and with his absorption into such characters as the man and woman in 'A Game of Chess'. He has also repeated such lives across time and in many cities. Since Tiresias is the figure into which these others 'melt', let us examine the range of sexual experience such people have so that we may see of what memories Tiresias is compounded.

The analysis of sexual neurosis in *The Waste Land* is placed between two moments of tentative vision. The first is the moment of return from the hyacinth garden in 'The Burial of the Dead' (ll. 35–41). The second is the sailing incident in 'What the Thunder said' (ll. 418–22). Both are moments of possible psychological potency; neither, as it happens, is completely so.

The first incident is particularly lovely and acute, a vision of spring flowers, a colourful garden and a loved and responding girl. Growth, potency and water characterize it. Here is a picture of a world without a Waste Land, a place where consciousness of self is lost in 'the heart of light, the silence'. But this moment is not sustained, as the two allusions to Wagner tell us. We move from the boyish love-longing of the young sailor to Tristan lying wounded in his Waste Land castle by the desolate sea.

The second moment of possible vision also concerns the sea (see pp. 47 and 71–2). Here we have a picture of sailing (as an undergraduate, Eliot had been a keen amateur yachtsman) in which the unity of man and boat, sea and wind, is again a joyous loss of self-consciousness. Such a unity is compared to that between lovers. But notice how the analogy is presented in the conditional tense: 'your heart *would* have responded'. The suggestion is that it did not. Insight is only a vision of what might have been. The commands of the god of thunder (see pp. 122–3) do not automatically bring peace and potency.

It is important to bear these moments of partial vision in mind, for it is at least partly against them that we should measure the description of sexual failure in the rest of the poem: the desperate scene of fornication in 'The Fire Sermon', the two scenes of 'A Game of Chess' and other lesser but related incidents.

'A Game of Chess' presents the almost total collapse of contemporary sexuality. It does so by contrasting the surreal and neurotic horrors of an over-cultured world with the abysmal life of London's East End. In the opening section (ll. 77–138) a desperate scene takes place in a nightmare room in which perverted memories of Dido and Cleopatra merge with the crudity of Greek myth. Here is the culture of the past at its neurotic end. The world that once created great verse has collapsed into incoherent, stuttering conversation, full of menace and memory, jazz, hysteria and drugs. The scene in the East End pub, by contrast, shows a voluble world of talk about nothing except failed marriage and infidelity, malicious gossip and abortions. Proletarian culture offers nothing with which to offset the neurosis of the educated. Memories of *Hamlet* cross it (l. 172) to make its trivial nature all the more desolate.

As is made clear in 'The Fire Sermon', such cultural and emotional impotence is an enduring fact of human experience. After the incident with the clerk and the typist (glimpsed through the intuition of Tiresias in the context of all time) comes the passage about the Thames (ll. 266–306). Gone is the celebration of potency found in Spenser (see pp. 136–7). Instead, there is only pollution, the 'nonsense' of Elizabeth and Leicester and, finally, a failed modern affair which peters out into the desolate scene on Margate Sands. Potency has failed. Sex and spiritual health have been sundered to the detriment of both. Eliot had reinforced this idea earlier on when we saw Mr. Eugenides trying to solicit the Narrator (the sexually ambiguous Tiresias) by an offer of lunch and a 'dirty weekend' in Brighton (ll. 207–14). Here, in the hallucinatory city familiar from 'The Burial of the Dead', the frowsty merchant, the descendant of the traders who had once brought knowledge of the life-enhancing cult to England (see pp. 101–2), is now at one with the typist and the clerk. Sex is tawdry and the myths have died. As Gerontion asks: 'After such knowledge, what forgiveness?'

The Tiresias/Narrator figure turns to religious insight. He thinks of St. Augustine tormented by the burning lusts of Carthage until, through suffering, he discovered the pattern of God's mercy (see pp. 127–9). He thinks, too, of the Buddha finding his way beyond the fires of desire. It is to this moment that Tiresias's knowledge of the endless and repetitive experience of stale sex has brought him.

As we begin to see Tiresias in this way, ancient and exhausted, so we see also that he embodies something permanently dreadful in human experience: a psychological inertia, a neurosis that cannot be cured. Such is the sexual horror that underlies *The Waste Land*. It is an impotence trapped in its own compulsions, suffering and homesick for salvation. What better way to encapsulate it than through an ambiguous and exhausted figure from myth, a blind prophet who needs but cannot see salvation and whose experience of sexual breakdown provides – in Freud's terminology – the 'model' for his experience of religious collapse.

The quest for religious insight

> *God is dead! God remains dead! And we have killed him! How shall we comfort ourselves – we who are the greatest murderers of all?*
> *Nietzsche,* The Gay Science

Secure in the faith that he would later be reborn, the ancient Egyptians mourned the god of fertility whom they slew every year with the harvest. These ceremonies of Osiris (see p. 97) provided them with a pattern of death and resurrection, garnering and seedtime, Waste Land and plenty. Here, in the forms of ritual, were both a chance to participate in the cycle of nature and an assurance that the cycle itself would continue. Finally, by a daring simile that for many thousands of years fixed the shape of mankind's most treasured hopes, priests compared these patterns of life and death to the fact of human mortality and a longed-for resurrection.

By contrast, the intellectuals of modern Europe, mourning the god they had slain on the altars of Intellect and Progress, were assured of no such eternal afterlife. To them the death of God was a final, irreversible fact, and it called forth some of their most lurid rhetoric. In 1852, the poet Heine declared: 'Our heart is full of terrible pity. It is the old Jehovah himself preparing for death ... Can you hear the ringing of the bell? Kneel down, they are bringing the sacraments to a dying God.'

Probably the greatest prose-poet of 'the death of God' was the philosopher Friedrich Nietzsche. His classic of propaganda for the new atheism is to be found in *The Gay Science* (1882). Here, in a famous passage, he tells how a madman visits a city of mild-minded atheists who do not appreciate the spiritual drama with which they are involved. They laugh at the madman when he tells them he is searching for God and, when his outburst is over, they can only stare at him in dumb incomprehension. The significance of the death of God is beyond them.

To Nietzsche, the death of God must lie at the centre of all modern man's thinking. He recognized clearly that if, on the one hand, the end of religion freed man from ancient trammels, it meant, on the other, that the structure of morality and faith that had once sustained him could do so no longer. We need not look here to the future that Nietzsche predicted as a result of the death of God; rather, we should concentrate on his vivid and very shrewd expression of man's proper fear now that he is left alone with only his own powers to depend on. It is to an awareness of this that the madman tries to rouse his citizens. The imagery he uses is not unlike that with which Stetson is challenged in the last part of 'The Burial of the Dead'. Under it we should feel the madman's panic at the thought of a godless universe:

> Do we not feel the breath of empty space? Has it not become colder? Is more and more night not coming on all the time? Must not lanterns be lit in the morning? Do we hear anything yet of the noise of the grave diggers who are burying God? Do we not smell anything yet of God's decomposition – gods, too, decompose.

And it is just this fear that is already 'beginning to cast its first shadows over Europe'. To those perceptive enough to realize it, the death of God must make it seem 'as though some sun had just gone down, some ancient profound trust had been turned round into doubt'.

That 'trust', of course, was the pattern of European morality that had been reared on the foundations of faith. Now, with the collapse of faith, there can only be 'demolition, destruction, decline, overturning' – and, for many, panic. The analogies to *The Waste Land* are obvious. As Nietzsche wrote in his notebooks, the death of God is 'the most terrible news'. It results in an 'unbearable loneliness'. In lines that again prefigure the imagery of *The Waste Land* and its longing for ritual comfort, the madman asks: 'With what water could we purify ourselves? What festivals of atonement ... shall we need to invent?' Finally, Nietzsche foresees some terrified modern men (in other words, those who do not follow his own new morality of strenuousness) turning back to seek their dead God and loving the very serpents that dwell in his ruined temples.

Forty years before the publication of *The Waste Land*, one of the seminal minds of the modern world had thus given expression to the consequences of 'the death of God' and the dilemma it posed for modern man. Eliot's poem is a further exploration of this. We could perhaps see the contemporary characters in *The Waste Land* as the cousins of those in the city visited by Nietzsche's madman. They too are largely unaware of the full drama involved in spiritual collapse, but the awfulness of their world is riddled with fear and incoherence precisely because they are living in a time without gods.

It is this thought that returns us to the pattern of myth that is one of Eliot's chief rhetorical supports in the poem. As we have seen, the time immediately following the ritual sacrifice of the god in the vegetation cults was one of genuine fear and collapse, of mourning and destruction. The land had lost the means by which it might be redeemed. It was at one with the sterile domains of the Fisher King. This position is exactly comparable to the world of modern man now that he, too, is without a god. He lives in a time of abject blight, a time not only of sexual squalor but of spiritual fear and decay.

This is made clear in 'The Burial of the Dead' when we are taken through the desert, past the 'heap of broken images' to the promise of a vision of 'fear in a handful of dust'. There is here, quite simply, 'Nothing again nothing'. The leaves have withered, the wind blows over 'the brown land, unheard', while the mountains are tormented by 'dry sterile thunder without rain'. Even in the cities, life has collapsed or is threatened with destruction. The crowds of commuters are spiritually inert, figures from hell though they barely recognize it, and, with the collapse of psycho-sexual joy, men turn to other things. They consult Madame Sosostris, for example. Before them are dealt the cards which once symbolized an active and coherent life of the body and spirit and were supposedly the means of freeing the waters that would redeem the parched Waste Land. But this insight is now blinded and lost. Modern man is trapped in hysteria and neurotic repetition. There is nothing within him, it seems, by which he can be given access to a fuller life. He has only his own resources to rely on and these are spent. His world is endlessly self-referring. Wherever Tiresias turns, he sees only decay and the denial of life, an impotence that has been known through all the ages. Such is modern nihilism, the world of 'nothing' where nothing connects. Only something beyond desire, an order beyond man, can sustain him – or, at least, has sustained him in the past.

There are two alternatives: 'death by water', the literal extinguishing of the burning self and the slow extinction of memories of human life; or the desperate search to 'set my lands in order'. The last part of *The Waste Land* is the most moving cry for vision, the Good Friday of the modern soul, when Christ (the Hanged God) has been slain and man is left alone with his desperate and incoherent energies, energies which are nearing exhaustion and which (in the absence of the spirit) are almost entirely physical: 'agony in stony places', dry sweat, nightmare landscapes where 'one can neither stand nor lie nor sit', a place, above all, of noise and thirst. The exhausted body houses a mind at the end of its tether, a mind tormented, hallucinating and riven with the forces of chaos. 'Hooded hordes' threaten the horizons, and ghastly visions screech out the end of the world. We have already traversed the city of dreadful night, seen the life-denying routines of work and sex, peeped into boudoirs and bed-sits, been anguished, solicited and despised. We have crossed the deserts of the Fisher King and witnessed the passion of the death of God (ll. 322–30). We have come, finally, to the Grail chapel and found it empty.

Now comes the moment of partial vision:

> ... a flash of lightning. Then a damp gust
> Bringing rain

The thunder booms out its three commandments: *datta, dayadhvam, damyata,* 'give, sympathize, control'. With these comes the promise of rain. There is not, it should be noted, any actual downpour to fill the 'sunken' river and revive 'the limp leaves'. Redemption does not drop 'as the gentle dew from heaven'. The Waste Land remains barren. There is no automatic promise that it will be fed and watered 'by God's almighty hand'. Instead, there are the commandments that rely wholly on man's own strength. Disillusioned and exhausted as he is, unable to recognize a risen God and a pattern of salvation (ll. 359–65), his chapels empty and his mind near collapse, the Narrator is told to rely on what strengths remain to him. All he has to support him here are the incommunicable moments when love might have been shared (ll. 401–22). The Narrator is forced to turn back yet again on his own experience, the flickerings of his partial vision.

Unlike the knights of the Grail legend, we have not crossed the lands of the Fisher King and cured his wound, there is no progress to salvation and the rapturous ceremonies of the '*voix d'enfants, chantant dans la coupole*'. Instead, we are left with a heap of broken memories and the fragments of a smashed culture. We are left with commandments, actions we must perform out of our own sinking strength. There is no ritual pattern to take us in and tie us to a coherent universe. For all our searching we are left impotently in a ruined house and with 'the Peace which passeth understanding', it seems, beyond our grasp. God remains dead, but we can no longer be indifferent to this.

5. Ezra Pound: His Poetry and the Editing of the *Waste Land* Manuscript

> *... The poem [*Hugh Selwyn Mauberley*] seems to me, when you have marked the sophistication and great variety of the verse, verse of a man who knows his way about, to be a positive document of sensibility. It is compact of the experience of a certain man in a certain place at a certain time; and it is also a document of an epoch; it is genuine tragedy and comedy; it is, in the best sense of Arnold's worn phrase, a 'criticism of life'.*
>
> *T. S. Eliot,* Selected Poems by Ezra Pound (*1928*), *Introduction*

Pound's crucial influence on *The Waste Land* was, of course, the drastic process of editing to which he subjected the first manuscript (see below). We have noted, too, that Pound helped Eliot to find his way in London literary society and suggested that he move from the works of his Harvard period to satire. However, Pound's own poetry, and, in particular, *Hugh Selwyn Mauberley* (1919–20), is in many ways analogous to *The Waste Land*. Some description of it may help to clarify Eliot's work and place it in the context of shared poetic problems and their solution. It will also suggest something of the background to Pound's editing of Eliot's poem.

Eliot's high regard for *Hugh Selwyn Mauberley* is clear from the quotation at the head of this section. Eliot obviously thought of Pound's sequence of poems as a seminal work. In barest outline, the poems tell of an American poet, E. P., and his English parallel, Mauberley. Mauberley is the *fin de siècle* versifier rendered sterile by the artistic world in which he moves and by his own pursuit of an atrophied inner life. All this:

> Leading, as he well knew,
> To his final
> Exclusion from the world of letters.

Poetic sterility is thus a central theme of Pound's poem and is a crucial aspect of the Waste Land of modern culture – its vulgarity, prudishness and hypocrisy, which blight the sources of true art and call in their turn for something instant and second-rate, a cheap reproduction, prose rather than monuments to outlast time:

> The 'age demanded' chiefly a mould in plaster,
> Made with no loss of time,
> A prose kinema, not, not assuredly, alabaster
> Or the 'sculpture' of rhyme.

It is among such a confusion of values that the modern poet is forced to write. On the one hand, he knows and appreciates the great traditions of the past; on the other, he is faced with a tawdry, desiccated age of shoddy tastes and feeble desires. This is precisely the cultural collapse that Eliot investigates in *The Waste Land*; and, just as Eliot ranges over the past only to find 'a heap of broken images', so Pound looked to, among other places, nineteenth-century France and the impersonal, elite, high-minded craftsmanship of Gautier, Baudelaire and Flaubert for his models of artistic rectitude. These writers, too, had faced the bewildering banality of bourgeois culture and had cultivated style, craftsmanship and trenchant observation as a means of defence.

As in Eliot also, we find in *Hugh Selwyn Mauberley* an analysis of two matters that both Pound and his pupil felt as crucial to their times: the First World War (see pp. 9–10) and the repressed, timorous nature of modern sexuality. Both are aspects of the modern Waste Land.

Pound's descriptions of the horrors of the war are particularly moving. He was aware of its sheer horror in a way that was different from and perhaps more powerful than Eliot's. He recognized the bravery of the soldiers and the destruction of the old order of patriotism and honour that the war produced. He realized further that such a defence of culture as the war had been was particularly ironic since the culture that was being defended had gone rotten:

> There died a myriad,
> And of the best, among them,
> For an old bitch gone in the teeth,
> For a botched civilization ...

Part of the reason for this cultural decay was the atrophying of sexual life. Woman – in Pound's view – was no longer the 'conservatrix' of the erotic, the true souce of inspiration in poetry. His own translations and concern with Latin love poetry (particularly Propertius), with Provençal lyric (see pp. 30–31) and with the literatures of France and China make this connection clear, but, in *Hugh Selwyn Mauberley*, sexuality is seen as suffocated by the *petit bourgeoisie*:

> ... in Ealing
> With the most bank-clerkly of Englishmen?

Lady Valentine in the twelfth section of the poem is incapable of 'a durable passion' for her poet. For her, poetry is a rather uncertain social pleasure and 'a possible friend and comforter'. She has relinquished her role as the muse, the inspirer and the object of great verse. In her world of preciousness and hesitation, she is

> Doubtful, somewhat, of the value
> Of well-gowned approbation
> Of literary effort . . .

The old sources of passion and coherence have gone. The modern world wants the commonplace and, in a time of commercialism and journalism, knows very well how to promote the second-rate and make a lot of money out of it – the satire on Mr. Nixon (Arnold Bennett), the successful hack and self-publicist 'in the cream gilded cabin of his steam yacht', is devastating. Holding to meaningless and tentative subjectivities, the weak poet Mauberley is destroyed, while the repression of the erotic life leads very close to sterility for the stronger one too. Looking at the fakes and faded characters in the poem, one is reminded of another embattled American, the painter Mark Rothco, who defined such ways of life as this as 'the cruelty of the impotent who would extend their affliction universally'. In both *The Waste Land* and in the larger part of *Hugh Selwyn Mauberley*, it is just their success that we are forced to witness.

It had long been known that the version of *The Waste Land* published in 1922 had been edited by Ezra Pound and that Eliot's slightly later dedication to *il miglior fabbro* was an expression of his gratitude. For nearly fifty years it was assumed that whatever passages had been excised had been lost beyond recall. However, in 1968 the original draft came to light in New York and has subsequently been edited and printed.

Though the material we now have is of great interest in terms of a more detailed knowledge of Eliot's state of mind at the time of writing the poem, and though it also provides some interesting insights into the process of creating the work, it is clear that the effort which Pound put into reducing what he was later to call 'the longest poem in the Englisch langwidge [*sic*]' was wholly beneficial. A very small number of fine lines had to be lost in the process, but the many more that were discarded are uncouth and irrelevant. They add almost nothing to the deepest concerns of the poem; rather, they distract and sometimes even threaten to devalue the work. The majority are false starts.

The original title of the poem – *'He do the Police in different Voices,* – was taken from Dickens's novel *Our Mutual Friend* and helps to suggest the effect of the unedited version. It is essentially a series of poems rather than a single meditation and is overall far less coherent than the final published version. For example, the initial opening of 'The Burial of the Dead' is a weak description of a night on the town. Here is Sweeney in a top hat but deprived of his pathos, his poetry. The rhythm is limp and the drama virtually non-existent. Again, the false start to 'The Fire Sermon' is more revealing of Eliot's immediate and personal insecurities than of how, in the greatest parts of the poem, he gives these a universalized significance. Indeed, the contrast makes a particularly fascinating example of how the submerging of the individual talent in tradition did indeed strengthen Eliot's work. The discarded original lines are merely a pastiche of eighteenth-century heroic couplets. They reveal nausea in the face of female sexuality, a fear of what is seen as women's lubricious and trivializing natures (see pp. 21–3). They lack the sense of the horrifyingly grotesque which one finds in similar verses of Swift and the far more mature sense of genuine desperation in the first half of 'The Fire Sermon' that now remains. They seem more like the lashing out of a deeply troubled man, his attempt to flail the world with the violence of his symptoms, than the expression of a more universalized sense of failure in the lines that remain. There is too much of a suggestion in the rejected material of a psychological striptease. Here, for example, is a description of a frivolous socialite reading an eighteenth-century novel while on the lavatory:

> Leaving the bubbling beverage to cool,
> Fresca slips softly to the needful stool,
> Where the pathetic tale of Richardson
> Eases her labour till the deed is done.

The anti-Semitism in this section is also unpleasant and becomes particularly so in one of the satellite poems in the manuscript entitled 'Dirge'. This is a gross parody of Ariel's song in *The Tempest*, a wilfully sick inversion that appears especially unpleasant and crude when compared to the evocative use of Shakespeare's play in the main body of the final version.

'Dirge' certainly compares unfavourably with the haunting beauty of the published version of 'Death by Water', but the manuscripts reveal that this was originally far longer, a description of a disaster at sea being tacked on to the start.

The loss of a few lines in the original version of 'Death by Water' is to be regretted, as is also true of a fragment called 'The Death of the Duchess'. Nonetheless, a comparison of the *Waste Land* drafts with the final version reveals precisely how creative Pound's editing was. He discarded what was weak, finding it to be also largely irrelevant. With a sure, creative insight, he probed to the heart of the original and extracted from it the more coherent, more profound work that has long been seen as one of the crucial statements of twentieth-century life.

6. The Sources

We can say that it appears likely that poets in our civilization as it exists at present, must be difficult. *Our civilization comprehends great variety and complexity, and this variety and complexity, playing upon a refined sensibility, must produce various and complex results. The poet must become more and more comprehensive, more allusive, more indirect, in order to force, to dislocate if necessary, language into his meaning.*

Tradition ... cannot be inherited, and if you want it you must obtain it by great labour.

T. S. Eliot

In our brief study of Eliot's university days we saw something of the wide range of subjects in which he interested himself: the Greek and Latin classics; philosophy; French, German and English literature; Dante; and, a little later, primitive religion, Sanskrit and Indian philosophy. This was no dilettante study, the casual browsing through a score of books. It was a training which offered an American, young in years if not in mind, a panoptic view of western literary traditions and eastern religious values, and, in addition, it provided considerable intellectual rigour when it came to analysing their content. Given Eliot's concern with tradition, his belief in the superiority of received wisdom freshly experienced (see pp. 17–18 and 61–2), it is natural that it should be against this inheritance that he measured his contemporary world and found it lacking. We should recall that Eliot is pre-eminently not the poet of the spontaneous, the 'gut reaction'. He is not the individual cornering you with a tale of his own woes. The medium of his poetry is tradition and the past. These, he claimed, are our true perspectives on the present. It is for this reason that we should know something about his sources and, as Eliot would say, ourselves.

To be familiar with Eliot's sources is far more than a game of I spy – here is a reference to Baudelaire, here one to Dante, here another to fertility rites or the *Upanishads*. Mere cataloguing is a dull activity and, in the end, quite opposed to the nature of the poem. It is what the sources suggest that is important. We must know them for what they are, hear in them how other people in times and places far removed expressed their experience of the potent or the sterile, the liberating or the purgatorial, and expressed them in such a way that they speak for all times and all places.

There is no substitute for reading the sources. None of them is overly obscure. All that need to be are available in translation. The task of becoming an ever better reader of *The Waste Land* is the necessary one of strengthening one's grip on the past and thereby securing a view of the present. This can lead to the appreciation of many things: a variety of poetry and music, to history and the history of ideas. It will certainly lead to a fuller appreciation of the poem. The purpose of this section is to give some starting points and guidelines for such reading, some basic vocabulary of analysis.

Sir James Frazer: *The Golden Bough: Adonis, Attis, Osiris*

> *Taken altogether, the coincidences of the Christian with the heathen festivals are too close and too numerous to be accidental. They mark the compromise which the Church in the hour of its triumph was compelled to make with its vanquished yet still dangerous rivals.*
>
> *Sir James Frazer*

The Waste Land is particularly concerned with all-but-forgotten religious rites, the ways in which earlier men, terrified by the winter failing of nature, sought to restore her to life through sympathetic magic. They believed that if only they could imitate the pattern of death in the winter and resurrection at the spring, then they could ensure that the cycle of life would be truly maintained. They thought they could guarantee by the ceremonies at the heart of their religions that crops would grow, cattle be fertile, womenfolk bear children. They believed that blighted potency could indeed be restored if man were in harmony with his gods. Not for them, in the overwhelming need to survive, was the spiritless, casual sex of Sweeney at Mrs. Porter's, the spotty house clerk's one-night stand. Sexual potency and religious faith were one.

Eliot found an analysis of the fertility cults in Sir James Frazer's *The Golden Bough*, and in his Notes to *The Waste Land* he states how the twelve volumes of this work had 'influenced our generation profoundly'. That this was indeed the case is shown by the issue of a popular one-volume abridgement in 1922, the same year as Eliot's poem.

Eliot directs the reader to Frazer's accounts of Adonis, Attis and Osiris. These were the fertility gods of the ancient cultures of the eastern Mediterranean. Adonis (or, more properly, Tammuz) belonged to the Babylonians and the Syrians; Attis originated in Phrygia and his cult was widely taken up by the Roman Empire; Osiris was Egyptian. All three figures, whose worship was common to the sources of European culture, are essentially similar. They are the divine yet mortal lovers of the greatest of powers, the Mother Goddess who, as Ishtar, Cybele or Isis, personified the various potency of nature. It was the union of this goddess with her lover which ensured the fertility of the land. It was the death and sexual maiming of the god and his consort's subsequent search for him in the underworld that were the origins of winter and its infertility. The gods departed and the world was Waste Land. It was the belief of all their worshippers that by simulating the death and resurrection of the male – be he Adonis, Attis or Osiris – they could ensure the return of the goddess and hence the return of life to their land.

Although there were local variations in the worship of Adonis, the nature of his rites was substantially the same. There were, in addition, two great centres of his cult: one in Cyprus and a second at Byblus, the holy city of the Phoenicians. It is of the rites at this latter temple that we are reminded when Eliot talks of Phlebas the Phoenician and Mr. Eugenides the Smyrna merchant. It is they who are the link, however tenuous, with a people who elaborated the ceremonies which they believed could redeem the Waste Land of winter.

What form did the ceremonies take? The worship of Tammuz-Adonis is particularly interesting. In the religious literature of the Babylonians we read of his annual death and of how the Mother Goddess followed him to the underworld 'to the land from which there is no returning, to the house of darkness, where dust lies on door and bolt'. During this time the potency of the land was severely threatened, since the sexual functions of the animal and human kingdoms were wholly dependent on hers. In the dirges which the mourners sang over Tammuz's and Ishtar's departure we have an early picture of the Waste Land itself:

> A Tamarisk that in the garden has drunk no water,
>> Whose crown in the field has brought forth no blossom.
> A willow that rejoiced not by the water course,
>> A willow whose roots were torn up.
> A herd that in the garden had drunk no water.

Here indeed is the place

>> where the sun beats,
> And the dead tree gives no shelter, the cricket no relief
> And the dry stone no sound of water.

The revival of the dead god is equally interesting. The mourners of Adonis – who were chiefly women – made images of him and dressed them to resemble his corpse. At the great temple at Byblus, as the spring rain washed down the red earth from the mountains and so seemed to stain the river with his blood, the women carried out the corpse of Adonis as if for burial and threw it to the sea. The god was drowned, but it was believed that he rose again on the next day and ascended to heaven in the sight of his worshippers. Thus the fertility of the land was restored.

The similarity of this ceremony to the fourth section of *The Waste Land* – the elegy to the drowned Phoenician sailor – and to Madame Sosostris's warning to 'fear death by water' is clear. The image of the god ritually drowned by the Phoenicians ensured the restoration of the Waste Land, the return of fertility and rain. Now, in the enfeebled twentieth century, drowning is something to fear, or, at best, a lyrical interlude in a desert of pain. And the Phoenicians themselves are no longer traders spreading knowledge of their life-ensuring cult. Mr. Eugenides, the Smyrna merchant, merely offers gaudy rewards in return for casual sex. The ritual is potent no more.

The youthful Adonis was gored in the thigh by a boar. Sexual maiming is even clearer in the cult of Attis. His rites – and those of the Mother Goddess Cybele – were widely spread through the Roman Empire, being celebrated from Africa to Bulgaria and known from the earliest times to at least the fourth century, when they were observed by St. Augustine in Carthage. Their form was as follows. On 23 March a pine tree was carried into the temple of Cybele. This was wrapped like a corpse and decorated with violets. An effigy of Attis was then tied to it. On the third day of the ceremony, the Day of Gore, the high-priest of the cult slashed his arms and presented his blood as an offering. Frazer's description of the rest of the ceremony is too picturesque not to quote:

Nor was he alone in making this bloody sacrifice. Stirred by the wild barbaric music of clashing cymbals, rumbling drums, droning horns and screaming flutes, the inferior clergy whirled about in the dance with waggling heads and streaming hair, until, rapt into a frenzy of excitement and insensible to pain, they gashed their bodies with potsherds or slashed them with knives in order to bespatter the altar and the sacred tree with their flowing blood. The ghastly rite probably formed part of the mourning for Attis and may have been intended to strengthen him for the resurrection ... Further, we may conjecture, though we are not expressly told, that it was on the same Day of Blood and for the same purpose that the novices sacrificed their virility. Wrought up to the highest pitch of religious excitement, they dashed the severed portions of themselves against the image of the cruel goddess. These broken instruments of fertility were afterwards reverently wrapped up and buried in the earth or in subterranean chambers sacred to Cybele, where, like the offering of blood, they may have been deemed instrumental in recalling Attis to life and hastening the general resurrection of nature, which was then bursting into leaf and blossom in the vernal sunshine.

Frazer adds a further interesting conjecture: that the dummy represent-
ing Attis was once the high-priest himself who was actually slain on the
sacred tree. He goes on to draw a parallel with Norse mythology, and
describes how, in the sacred grove at Upsala, human victims dedicated
to Odin were hanged or stabbed and then tied to a tree and ritually
wounded with a spear. It was from this ceremony that the god derived
his name of the Lord of the Gallows or the God of the Hanged.

Before we associate this figure with that in Madame Sosostris's Tarot
pack (ll. 54–5) and, following Eliot's clue, with the hooded figure in
'What the Thunder said' (ll. 359–65 and note to l. 46), we should look
at some of the inferences which Frazer draws from his material, inferences
which account for the significance that *The Golden Bough* held for Eliot's
contemporaries. We may do so by examining Osiris.

The third deity in the group that Eliot directs us to is the Egyptian
god Osiris. At the simplest level he was a vegetation god – a sort of
Egyptian John Barleycorn who was buried during seedtime so that he
would rise again with the corn. When the corn was cut, it was the custom
of the reapers to beat their breasts and lament over the first sheaf while
calling on Isis, the consort of the god whom they were now putting to
death. However, the particular significance of Osiris lies less in his
function as a fertility god – the guarantor that the Waste Land of harvest
will be redeemed – than in the great leap of metaphor by which a god
of fertility came to be seen as a god of human resurrection. Frazer turns
here to archaeology. Just as images of Osiris were buried in the fields
to ensure the rebirth of the corn, so seed-covered models of his carefully
mummified form were buried in human tombs as a pledge of resurrection
to an afterlife. As the corn would rise again, so too, it was believed, would
the human body. Frazer comments: 'From the sprouting of the grain the
ancient Egyptians drew an augury of human immortality. They are not
the only people who have built the same lofty hopes on the same slender
foundation.'

The tone of the donnish irony is significant. Frazer's lengthy charting of
these ancient rites – which he knew too intimately wholly to deride –
points time and again to the more than passing resemblance which they
bear to the Christian mystery of a divine man who died and rose again
for the benefit of mankind. It is in the spiritualization of such pagan
rituals that the analogy is clearest.

One example must suffice. The public ceremony surrounding the death
and resurrection of Attis was accompanied by a series of more secret
rites whose probable aim was to bring the worshipper into a closer communion with his god. These ceremonies included a sacramental meal and
a baptism in blood. For the baptism, the devotee descended into a pit

which was covered by a wooden grating. On to this was led a flower-decked bull, which was then slaughtered with a consecrated spear. His hot innards poured down through the grating and deluged the worshipper below. He then eagerly showered himself in the blood of sacrifice and finally emerged to the joyous admiration of his fellows as a soul 'who had been born again to eternal life and had washed away his sins in the blood of the bull'. The ceremony took place concurrently with the public rites of Attis – in other words, on or about 23 March, which was also the most ancient date of the Christian Easter. The centre of the cult was Rome, and at the beginning of the seventeenth century, when St. Peter's was being enlarged, many inscriptions were found to prove that the basilica of the Pope had more anciently been the sanctuary of Cybele.

It is small wonder that the similarity between the two beliefs should have been a cause of controversy, the pagans suggesting that Christian myth was merely an imitation of the cycle of their own god – who was, after all, the elder – and the Christians retaliating that the worship of Attis was the work of the Devil, whose cunning was such that on this supreme occasion he had inverted the order of nature to make it only seem that Attis had come first. What is particularly important to remember, however, is that certain very early groups of heretical Christians saw their own faith as the fulfilment of the promises of the earlier one and, in the absence of a full liturgy, used pagan ceremonies as a means of contact with the godhead. When we come to examine the Grail legends, we shall see how important these heretical Christians were considered to be in maintaining the traditions of fertility rites and vegetation myths.

As far as *The Waste Land* as a whole is concerned, the salient points are these. Eliot – whose own conversion to Christianity was still some five years away – was aware of the spiritual and psychological needs that a complex of ancient fertility cults (analogous to Christianity in ritual purpose if not in ethical content) had once fulfilled. These cults had centred around the union of a Mother Goddess with a divine but mortal male whose death and sexual maiming caused her to withdraw from the world and so impose the sterility of a winter Waste Land. In the most ancient civilizations, particularly those of the eastern Mediterranean, it was believed that the dead god could be resurrected by a process of sympathetic magic which may once have involved a real victim for whom an effigy was later substituted. Among the Phoenicians, this deity was named Adonis and his resurrection took place after a ritual drowning. In addition, the cult began to take on a metaphysical dimension which concerned not simply the sexual regeneration of life but also the spiritual rebirth of believers. There was, in other words, a direct connection between the redemption of the parched Waste Land, and the restoration of potency to animals and of eternal life to man. In *The Waste Land* itself, this process of revitalization is a half-felt, half-remembered need that can no longer be satisfied. When the risen god appears – be he Attis, Odin or Christ – he cannot be recognized for what he is (see ll. 359–65). Instead, we are locked in the sterile period of mourning for a banished god but can believe in no imminent resurrection. Sex has been devalued, ritual is a cheat, and the spiritual is confounded in the psychosomatic. The best are those who know only how sick they are, and for them the revival of spring is an infinitely painful matter.

Jessie L. Weston: *From Ritual to Romance*

> *After upwards of thirty years spent in careful study of the Grail legends and romances I am firmly and entirely convinced that the root origin of the whole bewildering complex is to be found in the vegetation ritual, treated from the esoteric point of view as a life-cult, and in that alone.*
>
> *Jessie L. Weston*

A second important source of Waste Land imagery can be found in those tales of the Knights of the Round Table which concern the quest for the Holy Grail. There are a great number of these, and some, like the *Parzival* of Wolfram von Eschenbach, are masterpieces of medieval literature. The common elements of the tales are hugely compelling, and if the narratives of the Middle Ages were to influence such nineteenth-century artists as Tennyson and Wagner, the other work that Eliot refers us to – Jessie L. Weston's *From Ritual to Romance* – claims to find the origins of Grail imagery in the vegetation cults analysed by Frazer.

The medieval narratives surround the Grail with the utmost mystery, the terror that veils an ultimate spiritual truth. Women were debarred from knowledge of it, and only the unwedded and preferably virgin male, shuddering and breathless, could learn more of its secrets. To do so, he must have undergone a quest that strained his qualities to the utmost. In some unspecified way, the Grail provided the Food of Life, and to be worthy of receiving it the hero must have passed through a Waste Land similar to the Valley of Death.

In its earlier versions at least, the purpose of the quest was not to secure the well-being of the hero, be he Parsifal (see l. 202) or Gawain. The main object was to restore to health the king who was the guardian of the Grail and whose sickness, for some unexplained reason, had reduced his kingdom to the desolation of drought and death: to a Waste

Land. It is Weston's argument that it was the sickness of the guardian that had reduced his country (not the other way around) and that it was the redemption of him and his blighted realm that was the central and most significant motif of the stories. She cites one particularly vivid description of the sterility which the guardian king's illness had caused:

> ... here no fertile seed is sown,
> Neither peas nor grain are grown,
> Never a child of man is born,
> Mateless maidens sadly mourn,
> On the trees no leaf is seen
> Nor are the meadows growing green,
> Birds build no nests, no song is sung,
> And hapless beasts shall bear no young,
> So is it while the sinful king
> Shall evil on his people bring.

As the Waste Land of the Grail legends is due to the sickness of the Grail's guardian, and as, in addition, it is the restoration of him and the consequent revival of his realm that is the central issue of the tales, some further insight into his origin are desirable. Who, we may ask, is he?

He is the Fisher King, and fish, as Weston makes clear, are ancient symbols of fertility. Eliot's references to him at once spring to mind: the Narrator fishing in the 'dull canal', the man with three staves in Madame Sosostris's Tarot pack whom Eliot associates 'quite arbitrarily' with the Fisher King himself. However, we should trace the relation which Weston sees between this figure and Attis and Adonis before we can place the Grail imagery of *The Waste Land* in its full context. When we have done so, we shall see that what Weston and Eliot were concerned to present was the long and eventually Christianized tradition of wisdom which recognized sterility, knew how it could be overcome, but which was now exhausted and all but forgotten.

Weston relates the Tammuz-Adonis cult of Frazer to her own Grail legends by associating the guardian of the Grail with the priest-kings who, in the very earliest days of the vegetation cults, actually played out the role of the dying god. She also makes it explicit that the wound suffered by Adonis was in his genitals, and adds that this accounts for the infertility of the land. By association, the wound of the Fisher King was similar. Weston supports these analogies by drawing further parallels between events in the Grail castle – the dead or wounded ruler on his litter, the sterility of his kingdom, the vociferous lamentation of his women and, in one case, the appearance of a maiden who had shaved her hair – and the rituals of the vegetation cults in which the dying hero was similarly presented surrounded by weeping women who had shaved their heads and who loudly mourned the death of their god. Such similarities between Tammuz-Adonis, on the one hand, and the Fisher King, on the other, are sufficient in Weston's view to call the figures one and the same.

There remains the problem of how and why the Fisher King and the Grail legend lodged so persistently in the common memory and became associated with the Christian chivalry of medieval Europe; of how, in terms of *The Waste Land*, a pagan vegetation ceremony could be associated with a Christian knight's approach to the Chapel Perilous, a place which in the legend is one of great fear and testing, but in *The Waste Land* is an apparently empty husk, a cheat:

> In this decayed hole among the mountains
> In the faint moonlight, the grass is singing
> Over the tumbled graves, about the chapel
> There is the empty chapel, only the wind's home.
> It has no windows, and the door swings,
> Dry bones can harm no one.

The answer that Weston provides relates to the division which Frazer noted between the public cults of Adonis, Attis and Osiris, and the secret, esoteric mysteries in which the novice was led to a deeper communion with his god (see pp. 97–8). It was these secret rites, Weston believed, which provided the Grail legend with its symbolism of a mystic meal, the Food of Life served in a sacred vessel. It was also in these esoteric aspects of the Attis cult that the earliest heretical Christians participated, since, eager for established ritual, they believed that through them they could most readily approach God. It was on this level of an initiation into solemn mysteries that the cult of Attis could be equated with that of Christ. Both, as we have seen, shared a kinship of esoteric ritual and, as Weston states: 'When Christianity came upon the scene it did not hesitate to utilize the already existing medium of instruction, but boldly identified the Deity of Vegetation, regarded as the Life Principle, with the God of the Christian Faith.'

How did these experiments in mystic ritual become the stuff of medieval romance? Weston believed (probably correctly) that mystery religions were brought to England by three groups of people: Phoenician merchants, the Asiatic slaves of the Roman conquerors and, thirdly and most importantly, the Roman legionaries themselves. The outward aspects of the mystery religions lasted for many years, but were finally quashed when a Christianity neatly trimmed of dangerous pagan trappings became the official religion of the Empire. The cults' esoteric, mystical aspect nonetheless survived 'and was celebrated in sites removed from the centres of population – in caves, and mountain fastnesses; in islands, and on desolate sea-coasts'. Perhaps this was so. Certainly, it is the basis on which Weston builds her next (and rather unlikely) hypothesis.

She takes a story retold in three Grail romances of how a British king outraged one of the maidens who lived in the secret hills and then, along with his knights, stole the golden cups with which these women offered hospitality to travellers. In Weston's interpretation, the rape of these maidens represents an actual outrage committed by a local chieftain on the priestesses of the vegetation cults. As a result, the springs dried up, the court of the Fisher King disappeared and the land lay waste for a thousand years. Finally, a descendant of a guardian of the outraged maidens came to Arthur's court (Weston firmly believed in Arthur as a historical figure) and told him of the Fisher King, the Grail and how the land might be fertile once more. A rite which from immemorial time had been known as the greatest test in which a man could engage thus became the goal of Arthur's Christianized knights.

Weston proposes that the earliest writers of the Grail stories actually knew the real character of their material, 'knew the Grail cult as Christianized mystery', and deliberately recast it in the form of an Arthurian romance. Only later, when this esoteric knowledge was more or less lost, did the Grail legend take on the element of pure romance that we find in such writers as Malory.

Thus, in brief, what had happened was this: the rituals of the vegetation cults had been brought to England. The public ceremonies were replaced by Christianity, but the esoteric rites remained as the secret knowledge of a scattered people. There was a long tradition which associated these mysteries with Christianity and which also claimed that initiation into them was the greatest adventure a man could undergo. Medieval writers, presenting the court of King Arthur as the perfect example of Christian chivalry, knew something about the ancient mysteries and decided to portray a version of them as the greatest quest a Knight of the Round Table could undertake. As time wore on, the real nature of the mysteries was largely forgotten, but their trappings remained as strange, alluring details that could be explored in a number of ways. Weston's research, based on Frazer, traced the origins of these details back beyond the Middle Ages and early Christianity to the fertility cults of the ancient world. In important respects, the Fisher King is Adonis himself. In the Grail legends, Christianized mystery is at one with the pagan world.

A single example of this process of Grail romance looking back to pagan ritual must suffice: the story of the quester at the Perilous Chapel

and Cemetery. This is the scene which Eliot recreates in the last section
of *The Waste Land* (ll. 384–94).

In the best medieval versions, the Chapel Perilous deserves its name.
Gawain discovers it at a crossways in the forest and enters it to avoid
a storm. He finds on the bare altar a great gold candlestick with a burning
taper. From the altar window emerges a black hand which extinguishes
the candle. A terrible sound of lamentation then shakes the building.
Gawain makes the sign of the cross and rides from the chapel to find
the weather calm again. Similar mysteries surrounded the Perilous
Cemetery. In Weston's view, these stories, so elegantly sinister in their
medieval form, represent an initiation test connected to the mystery
rituals, an initiation into the secrets of life in which contact with fear
and death was of the greatest importance. Certainly, the connection
between the Grail and the Chapel Perilous is strongly made by the
medieval writers, and it is reasonable to suppose that such a test might
well have been exacted before entry to the Grail castle itself, the
subsequent redemption of the Fisher King, and knowledge of the far
greater mysteries that the Grail itself enshrined.

In *The Waste Land*, the beautifully sinister chapel is empty. There is
no candle, no Black Hand, no insight into the creative forces of natural
life. The Chapel Perilous is the extreme point of *The Waste Land*, high
and desolate in the dry mountains. Nonetheless, as we have seen (see
pp. 46–7), it is also a place of at least partial illumination.

Taken together, Frazer and Weston's work provides a startling insight
into a long tradition – at first pagan and then lightly Christianized –
of the Waste Land redeemed. Across the informed reader's mind passes
a colourful yet disorderly procession of eunuch priests and knights-at-
arms, fabulous temples and ruined chapels, prayer, lamentation and
sacrifice. He may feel, however fleetingly, contact with a religion much
older than Christianity, or, more precisely, a spiritual homesickness. Once
there was potency and the means of ensuring its continuance. Now the
neurotic ego is stranded in the desert with only broken promises for
company. Well-being was once guaranteed by ritual. Sexual love and
spiritual health were one. Now the voices of the past are a deformed
echo: Madame Sosostris blindly touting devalued gods, Mr. Eugenides
offering bribes in return for a similacrum of love, the grass singing by
the empty chapel. As the Narrator hears and sees these things, he is at
one with the maimed guardian of the Grail. His suffering is unredeemable.
It is therefore pointless. But so inured has he become to it that even
the slightest stirrings of life are painful (ll. 1–7). All he can do is sit
and survey the potent past of which he knows himself to be the bankrupt
inheritor.

Tarot Cards

> *The Tarot speaks in the language of symbols, the language of the*
> *unconscious, and when approached in the right manner it may open*
> *doors into the hidden reaches of the soul.*
> *Alfred Douglas,*
>   The Tarot: The Origins, Meaning and Uses of the Cards

From Ritual to Romance contains a brief description of the Tarot, but
Eliot's Notes tell us that he was unfamiliar with the 'exact constitution'
of the pack and he certainly put into Madame Sosostris's hands cards
of his own devising. It is impossible to guess precisely how much Eliot
did know about the Tarot, though it was clearly more than he derived
from Weston, who does not mention a figure as crucial to Eliot as the
Hanged Man. Since this is the case, a brief description of the pack and
its use in fortune-telling may be useful so that we can have a more
informed idea of how Eliot uses it.

The Tarot is a pack of seventy-eight cards. Fifty-six form the Lesser
Arcana, which is divided into four suits: Batons (Eliot's 'staves'), Cups,
Swords and Coins. These are the source of present-day playing cards.
The remaining twenty-two cards are the Greater Arcana and each depicts
a symbolic figure or scene. This group includes the Wheel of Fortune
and the Hanged Man. The cards were known in western Europe by the
late fourteenth century, but their origins are obscure. They contain
elements of various heretical Christian, Celtic, Norse and Islamic
imagery. They also seem to refer to various important aspects of Grail
symbolism – in particular, the Grail itself and the spear of Longinus.
Weston sees Egyptian and Chinese elements in them and thought the
Tarot may have been introduced from India by the gypsies. So wide a
range of possibilities means that it is unrealistic to make any final choice
of origin.

In terms of Eliot's use of the Tarot and Jessie L. Weston, the main
insights that he may have derived from *From Ritual to Romance* are the
suggestions, first, that the images of the Major Arcana were a group
of fertility symbols connected with ancient ritual, and, secondly, that
'the original use of the "Tarot" would seem to have been, not to foretell
the future in general, but to predict the rise and fall of the waters which
brought fertility to the land'. Such ideas were clearly very useful. Weston's
interpretation of the Tarot – which subsequent research has not borne
out – related the cards to the chief theme and image of *The Waste Land*:
the idea of infertility in all its forms and the water which, were man
in harmony with nature, would return prosperity and growth. In Madame
Sosostris's hands the Tarot cards are nothing of the sort. Snivelling over

her 'wicked pack', her wisdom is blind and fraudulent. She debases what she sees and also sees imperfectly. She does not find the Hanged Man and tells her querent to fear the death by water which provides the most lyrical moment in the poem, a pointer back to the revitalizing fertility of the vegetation cults. Previously, she had told him that the 'drowned Phoenician Sailor' was his own especial card.

In many respects, the consultation with Madame Sosostris is a jumble. It is an example of how the present has debased its inheritance and de-valued what were once the forces of life. For example, Madame Sosostris cannot see what the one-eyed merchant carries on his back, though Eliot indicates in his Notes that the card is a foretaste of Mr. Eugenides and we may thus suppose that what he carries is some suggestion of the rich Phoenician past to which he and Madame Sosostris are blind.

If we look at the consultation in more detail, some further points emerge. For example, in the most general form of Tarot reading, the first card indicates the dominant features of the querent's present circumstances. Here the card is the drowned Phoenician Sailor. Madame Sosostris actually states that this is the querent's own card, and it is fair to assume that the many associations that attach to it (the card is not, it should be noted, an obvious member of the traditional pack) do indeed say a great deal about his present state.

Madame Sosostris also mentions two cards from the Major Arcana: the Wheel and the Hanged Man. It may be a matter of some dispute how precisely the traditional meanings of these cards apply to *The Waste Land*, but before looking at these we should bear in mind that when actually being used the cards may come out upside down from their previous shufflings. If they are reversed, instead of presenting symbols of the quest for enlightenment, they tell of the dangers and difficulties that the querent may experience.

The Wheel of Fortune traditionally represents the point in a person's life when a major new phase is to begin. He is now free from the ties of society and has entered the period when he must directly confront the contents of the unconscious mind, a journey into doubt and night where the ego is no longer in control, nothing is constant, nothing certain. In the words of Alfred Douglas:

The second half of the quest has now begun. Examining the inner world of dreams and visions with the light of his intuition, the Hermit observes the strange images that rise before him from the depths. The sinking of his mind beneath the threshold of normal awareness allows unconscious material to rise above the surface.

When the card appears reversed, the surrender to the unconscious entails adversities which can only be endured until the Wheel has come full circle.

The Hanged Man again symbolizes that reversal of aims and values which should accompany the second half of life. The card itself represents a youth hanging upside down from a gibbet, his face calm and collected. The card suggests surrender to the laws of the universe, freedom from the ego. Reversed, it implies the disaster that comes from refusing to accept the unconscious, the triumph of materialism which is a form of defeat. In his Notes, Eliot tells how he associates this card with the Hanged God of Frazer and the passage in 'What the Thunder said' (ll. 359–65) which depicts Christ's appearance to the disciples on the road to Emmaus. Douglas again comments interestingly on the Hanged Man:

... The God Attis was hung in effigy each year on a pine tree. The tree is a symbol of the mother as the source of all sustenance; those who die on the tree are therefore being reunited with their source, through which they may be reborn into new life. By sacrificing his life the Hanged Man opens the way to his rebirth into the immortality of the spirit.

This is particularly illuminating, since it not only shows how shrewd was Eliot's association of the Hanged Man of the Tarot and the Hanged God of Frazer, but also presents the idea of rebirth into the immortality of the spirit which defines the reincarnated Christ and provides another link with Christian mystery and pagan rituals.

Eliot's comment that he associated the Man with the Three Staves 'quite arbitrarily' with the Fisher King may be taken at face value. Nonetheless, it is interesting that some versions of the card show a dolphin leaping from the sea, while others show a successful merchant staring out at his ships.

Eliot uses the Tarot scene as a particularly effective poetic device. He would have gathered from Jessie L. Weston that the cards were associated with fertility, the idea of freeing the waters and so redeeming the parched Waste Land. The cards also help him to connect his anthropological imagery – for example, to associate Frazer's Hanged God with Christ. By refusing to be constrained by the actual pack and by introducing such figures as Mr. Eugenides (who will later emerge as a character in his own right) and the milling crowds who are at once contemporary London commuters and the lost souls of the *Inferno* (see pp. 114–16), some of the main lines of the poem's imagery are established. Further, by introducing the drowned Phoenician Sailor, Eliot could point to other references in his poem, images connected to fertility and ritual drowning but which are at the same time more personal and elegiac. Above all, Eliot could suggest through this scene how the early twentieth century was only just in touch with its debased and trivialized past.

Much later in his life, when he had long been converted to Christian certainties, Eliot came to view such activities as Tarot reading as signs of spiritual collapsc. A passage in *The Dry Salvages* brings horoscopes, card reading, psychoanalysis and drug addiction together as props for the weak in the times

> When there is distress of nations and perplexity
> Whether on the shores of Asia, or in the Edgware Road.

Sophocles, Seneca, Ovid and the creation of Tiresias

> *There is no gentle breeze to cool the breasts*
> *Of fevered sufferers; no kind winds blow here.*
> *The Dog-Star scorches and the Lord Sun's fire*
> *Blows hot upon the Lion's heels. No water*
> *Runs in the rivers, fields are colourless.*
> *Dirce is dry, Ismenus thinly creeps,*
> *A shrunk stream barely moistening the sand.*
>
>

Seneca, Oedipus (*trans. E. F. Watling*)

A third source of Waste Land imagery may be found in the Oedipus plays. These also introduce us to a character central to Eliot's poem: Tiresias.

The tale of Oedipus is well known. His father, the ruler of Thebes, abandoned him at birth because of a prediction that he would be murdered by his son. The baby was saved by a Corinthian shepherd and brought up by the Corinthian king. When Oedipus was taunted for not resembling his supposed parents, he consulted the Delphic oracle, who drove him from her shrine, prophesying that Oedipus would kill his father and marry his mother. Horrified, Oedipus left Corinth and the couple he supposed were his parents. In a narrow defile he was insulted by his true father – whom of course he did not recognize – and he murdered him in anger. Oedipus then made his way to Thebes, where, having solved the riddle of the Sphinx and so freed his homeland from a curse, he was proclaimed king and married Jocasta, the widow of the father he had slaughtered. Plague descended on Thebes as a result of this incestuous relationship. Both Sophocles and Seneca open their Oedipus plays when the plague is at its height. Seneca in particular revels in the details of the Waste Land that Oedipus's crime has caused. Death and sterility abound, and the scenes reek with the smoke of funeral pyres. The particular interest of this set of Waste Land images is that they introduce us to the classical world and associate sterility with sexual sin.

One point should be borne in mind here. The civilization of classical Greece, particularly that of fifth-century Athens, is rightly regarded as

107

a pinnacle of human achievement. Many of its myths, however, are extremely cruel. The Oedipus story is no exception, and Eliot reacted strongly against such things. Stephen Spender tells how Lady Ottoline Morrell, a famous intellectual hostess of the thirties, discussed some photographs of fifth-century Greek statues with Eliot. For the majority of critics these sculptures are at the core of European ideas of beauty and decorum. They reminded Eliot, however, of snake worship, of the barbarous elements in Greek culture that so distressed him. To Eliot, Greek myths had no Wedgwood charm or English public-school respectability. They were truly horrific, something quite apart from the Latin Christian tradition with which he identified himself, and closer to the primitive menace of Conrad's *Heart of Darkness*.

In the plays, it is the prophet Tiresias who can reveal the truth to Oedipus and so hasten his tragedy. As he explains, it is Oedipus's sins of killing his father and marrying his mother – both innocently committed – that are responsible for the Waste Land of Thebes, and Oedipus himself is the curse who must be removed.

Tiresias is a further example of the ruthless side of Greek myth. Eliot quotes the following passage from the Latin poet Ovid in his Notes:

... it happened, so the story goes, that Jupiter put aside his weighty cares; mellowed by deep draughts of nectar, he indulged in idle banter with Juno, who shared his leisure, and teased her, saying: 'Of course, you women get far more pleasure out of love than men do.' Juno denied that this was true. They decided to ask the opinion of the wise Tiresias, for he had experienced love both as a man and as a woman.

Once, when two huge serpents were intertwining themselves in the depths of the green wood, he had struck them with his staff; from being a man he was miraculously changed into a woman, and had lived as such for seven years. In the eighth year he saw the same serpents again and said: 'If there is such potent magic in the act of striking you that it changes the striker to the opposite sex, I shall now strike you again.' So, by striking the same snakes, he was restored to his former shape, and the nature with which he was born returned.

He, then, was chosen to give his verdict in this playful argument, and he confirmed what Jupiter had said. Then, they say, Juno was more indignant than she had any right to be, more so than the case demanded, and she condemned the judge to eternal blindness. It is not possible for any god to undo the actions of another god, but in return for his loss of sight, the omnipotent father granted Tiresias the power to know the future and softened his punishment by conferring this honour upon him.

(trans. Mary M. Innes)

The use that Eliot makes of Tiresias is complex (see pp. 24–30 and 58–60) but, appropriately, he emerges at the mid-point of the poem, a suffering, ambiguous, timeless presence. But he has not come to stand in the middle of the Waste Land to cure it through revelation and tragedy. He can tell no truth, remove no curse. He does not prophesy what will eventually happen. Tiresias is no redeemer, even a despised one as he is in Sophocles. There can be no redemption in *The Waste Land*. Rather, the figure who appears is the blind and sexually ambiguous epitome of unredeemed human experience. This is what he personifies and also what he sees, or, since he is blind, 'perceives'. His knowledge and intuition are of futility.

The particulars of the scene which Tiresias first explicitly envisages are among the most immediate and moving in the poem: a picture of casual, loveless sex in a rented room (ll. 215–56). The intercourse of the typist and the house agent's clerk is a meaningless ritual described here by a blind and sexually ambiguous old man who subsumes into himself the futility of mankind's godless existence. Through Tiresias we see how the Waste Land of Thebes, its sterility and sexual sin, is at one with the Waste Land of modern London and, by association, with the other cities of the poem: Carthage, Vienna, Paris. Finally, all blighted sexuality is one, timeless and omnipresent:

> (And I Tiresias have foresuffered all
> Enacted on this same divan or bed;
> I who have sat by Thebes below the wall
> And walked among the lowest of the dead.)

Baudelaire

> *Là je vis, un matin, à l'heure, où sous les cieux*
> *Froids et clairs le Travail s'éveille, où la voirie*
> *Pousse un sombre ouragan dans l'air silencieux,*
>
> *Un cygne qui s'était évadé de sa cage,*
> *Et, de ses pieds palmés frottant le pavé sec,*
> *Sur le sol raboteux traînait son blanc plumage.*
> *Près d'un ruisseau sans eau la bête ouvrant le bec*
>
> *Baignait nerveusement ses ailes dans la poudre,*
> *Et disait, le coeur plein de son beau lac natal:*
> *'Eau, quand donc pleuvras-tu? quand tonneras-tu, foudre?'*
>
> *I saw there, one morning, at the time when beneath the cold, clear skies Toil wakes and road-menders send their dark uproar into the quiet air, a swan who had got out of its cage, and, rubbing the parched roadway with his webbed feet, trailed his white plumes on the raw ground. The*

> *creature opened its beak by a dry gutter, bathed its wings frantically*
> *in the dust and cried out, its heart full of longing for the lake where it*
> *had been born: 'Water, when will you rain down? Lightning, when will*
> *you rage?'*

> *Baudelaire,* Le Cygne

This picture of a bedraggled swan bathing in the dust and longing for rain comes from nineteenth-century Paris and the work of the greatest poet of the modern city, Baudelaire.

Baudelaire's life-work, *Les Fleurs du mal* (1857), is a long sequence of poems illustrating the cycle of human existence. It is a spiritual autobiography, the self-portrait of a man variously torn between appetite and apathy, yet constantly fighting to analyse himself with a ruthless finesse. But no simple formula adequately defines Baudelaire or his work. Only through repeated reading can we become familiar with its particular tensions, its varieties of escape into love, art, perversity and revolt. And from what was Baudelaire escaping? From *spleen*, the boredom that rots the soul and blunts the will. This is the Waste Land of psychological death that is a special menace to the overcultivated man in the modern city. But Baudelaire is not simply a dandy trying to impress us with his superior sensitivity. Like Hamlet's, his melancholy, his *spleen*, is deeply threatening. It is the life-in-death sterility of the modern Waste Land itself.

Paris provides the backdrop (the theatrical image is Baudelaire's own) for many of these poems. His Paris is a city of fogs and cat-haunted squares, a place of voluptuous love, a place from which to escape. It is a city of gimlet-eyed old women, pathetic in their widowhood, a place of spectres and the ever-changing detritus of modern life. Such ugliness is important. It is much easier, Baudelaire wrote, to dismiss everything in a period as offensive than to try and extract from it the mysterious beauty it may contain. The real task of the modern poet is to show how we are '*grands et poetiques*' even in our ties and patent-leather boots. Baudelaire uncovers this poetry partly by a scrupulous accuracy of detail. He rarely preaches direct, and when he does he is least effective. In *Spleen*, for example, when he wants to portray that complex and corrosive experience, he evokes a dank, cold January and a figure who once personified the month pouring great waves of death over the fog-bound suburbs. In his wretched room the poet's mangy cat is trying to bed down on the floor. Baudelaire hears the tolling of a bell and his wheezing clock, while, in a smelly pack of cards left him by some dropsical hag, the Knave of Hearts and the Queen of Spades gossip sinisterly about dead love. The picture is exact. There is no commentary, but the interest roused by the images has a tawdriness which is deeply felt. Here, in gloom and privacy, is the Waste Land of modern city life, what Baudelaire elsewhere calls 'the desert of *ennui*'.

Eliot cites Baudelaire in the opening and closing lines of the last section of the 'Burial of the Dead'. He relates his 'Unreal City' to the start of Baudelaire's *Les Septs Vieillards* ('The Seven Old Men'), which is a poem where terror in the gloomy modern city is powerfully evoked. At this point in Eliot's own poem (see p. 35) he is concerned to present London as a contemporary Waste Land, and Baudelaire's poem helps him to do this and to show also that London is at one with the sterile cities of the past (see pp. 51–2). Again, past times are seen as being continuously present.

Les Sept Vieillards begins with an evocation of the teeming city, a city full of dreams, where ghosts accost the passer-by in broad daylight. It is morning. A dirty yellow fog floods the city, and Baudelaire presents himself wandering through a noisy suburb. His mood is typical. His soul is weary, but he is steeling his nerves like a hero. The effect is at once to place the depressingly banal in an atmosphere of mystery and suspense, fatigue and bravery. Just as in the last section of 'The Burial of the Dead', so here the everyday becomes a threatening surrealist stage. There now appear on this seven old men, ragged, mendacious, bent at right-angles over their walking sticks. They chill the observer to the bone. The freaks have a look of eternity about them. Their ghoulishness is timeless. It is the same in Eliot. The two men who greet each other in 'The Burial of the Dead' are both London commuters in a brown dawn fog and, at the same time, the eternal ghostly types of the spiritually timid. At the close of *Les Septs Vieillards*, Baudelaire rushes home and locks himself in his room, sickened, terrified and depressed. His mind is hurt and disturbed by his enigmatic vision, this *danse macabre*.

Eliot closes the first part of his poem with a quotation from another Baudelaire work: 'You! hypocrite lecteur! – mon semblable, – mon frere!' This is the last line of *Au Lecteur*, the poem that is Baudelaire's manifesto.

We have seen that Baudelaire's poems work best when he is most concrete, most specific. Even his voluptuous images have precision. It is in this way that he most effectively conjures up emotions. However, because these emotions have been so deeply felt and analysed, the moods which Baudelaire presents are not mere sensations. The reader feels in them a moral significance. He wants to make clear to himself the full truth of these moods. For example, why is the dust-bathing swan so poignant? Why does the ungainliness and longing of a bird usually so serene provoke in us ideas of homesickness and disaffection, a feeling of would-be serenity hobbled by the world in which we live? Baudelaire is deliberately reticent about this. For him, beauty was something ardent yet sad which stimulated thought. He told Swinburne he was resolutely opposed to moral intentions in poems. A well-wrought poem naturally and strongly suggested its own *'morale'*. But what this might be is the reader's own affair. Precisely so. The best of Baudelaire's poems oblige us to understand them by examining ourselves. Baudelaire makes this clear in *Au Lecteur*.

The greater part of the poem is a moral diatribe, an analysis of human failings that reads like a highly original sermon. It is melodramatic and in places deliberately offensive. As we shall see, its effect hinges on its last line, the line which Eliot quotes.

Baudelaire begins by saying we are warped by stupidity, error, sin and small-mindedness. This is a subtle combination. Here are the traditional faults joined to the disarmingly petty and particular. Such an analysis is appropriate in the context of *The Waste Land*, since it is precisely as the spiritually petty that Eliot presents his London commuters, his representative modern men. To Baudelaire, too, we are all spiritual cowards, unaware that triviality is our greatest sin. To paraphrase him, we are blind to the horror as we descend through stinking gloom, our will-power sapped while we seize our furtive pleasures like a penniless lecher nibbling at the breast of an old tart. There are no great sins for us. Our souls are not big enough for them. We are destroyed by our own triviality. Our brains are a seething orgy of hyena voices and bestial gruntings among which one voice is stronger than the rest. It is not frenzied. It utters no savage cries, but it could swallow up the world in its yawn. This king of the menagerie of vice is Boredom – *l'Ennui*, *Spleen*. Baudelaire shows *Ennui* yawning as he smokes his pipe. With a reluctant tear in his eye he gloats over the wreck of his hopes. Boredom knows that all human aspirations are finally pointless, that they end in death and despair.

Of nothing is this truer than human love. The heart sets out with high hopes. In *Un Voyage à Cythere* (Cytherea is the island of Venus) Baudelaire compares the heart to a bird soaring around the rigging. As the ship draws closer to the island, however, the place of delight turns out to be a cheat. The island of love – once a flower-sweet grove – is a barren, rocky desert, an infertile outcrop at the centre of which the rotten corpse of a hanged man is pecked by hideous birds of prey. This figure the poet then recognizes as himself. Here are corruption and suffering. The end of sex is disgust. And it is this image of a gallows that Boredom is dreaming about in *Au Lecteur*. There is no redemption through love. Taken over by spiritual and psychological death, modern man ceases to strive and relishes his sterile end.

The contemporaries of Baudelaire were meant to feel outraged by all this – the images in the poem are still sufficiently nauseating – but they are not allowed to get away with feeling huffily superior. They might try and turn angrily from Boredom, but Baudelaire will not let them. You too, the reader, he says, are familiar with this fantastic monster *Ennui*: you hypocritical reader, fellow man, my brother. Right at the end of the poem we are inveigled into an unwilling conspiracy. We realize that we too have relished the corruption of sex, and now we are obliged to examine ourselves. After the sermon, confession can begin.

This is just the effect Eliot suggests. The Narrator calls out to the hurrying Stetson and corners him with a challenge. He taunts him with images of death and resurrection, with all the fear and sterility of modern life that Stetson would prefer to forget as he hurries to his office. But the Narrator draws him into facing the spiritual blindness which is the Waste Land of the modern world.

Dante

> *We feel that if the classic is a really worthy ideal, it must be capable of exhibiting an amplitude, a catholicity ... which are fully present in the medieval mind of Dante. For in the* Divine Comedy, *if anywhere, we find the classic in a modern European language.*
>
> T. S. Eliot, What is a Classic?

Of the great philosophical poets, Dante influenced Eliot most persistently. Perhaps this was more marked after Eliot's conversion to Christianity, but even in *The Waste Land* Dante provided Eliot with incidents against which to measure the moral bankruptcy of his times.

When we talk of Dante we usually mean the *Divine Comedy*, the work he wrote after his exile from Florence in 1302. In the three sections of this, Dante portrayed the afterlife in Hell, Purgatory and Paradise. It tells us a great deal about *The Waste Land* that Eliot was here able to use only the first two of Dante's books: the *Inferno* and the *Purgatorio*. Heaven is closed to him. In the spiritual sterility which he describes, there is as yet no place for faith in the redeeming Christ, for beatitude and the rituals of salvation. Eliot's subject is suffering.

Dante's poem is both immensely long and enormously complex. It is also the most rigorously patterned work of western poetry. The place of each incident is crucially important, while the unfolding of the whole presents a vast panorama of the Christian experience. Its argument cannot be usefully paraphrased in a short space, and only a full reading can begin to suggest Dante's unique combination of philosophy and vivid, concrete detail. As Eliot himself wrote in his essay on the poet in *The Sacred Wood* (1920):

> It is one of the greatest merits of Dante's poem that the vision is so nearly complete; it is evidence of this greatness that the significance of any single passage, of any of the passages that are selected as 'poetry', is incomplete unless we ourselves apprehend the whole.

With this in mind, we will look here at Eliot's particular references and try to suggest something at least of their general significance. We will begin with the *Inferno*.

Dante's poem begins on Good Friday in 1300, and his journey through the three regions takes place during the rest of the Holy Week of that year. He himself is thirty-five – half-way through his life – and at the start of the poem he is lost in the dark wood of human sin and ignorance. In order to leave it, nothing short of a full knowledge of the Christian afterlife, or the state of man's soul from torpor to beatitude, is sufficient. Dante will have to descend through Hell and then climb up through Purgatory to Heaven and the abode of the blessed spirits. For the greater part of the first two stages of his journey his guide is Virgil. In the poem, the pagan Latin poet is the voice of reason and conscience, man's best supports in a world unredeemed by divine illumination. Virgil is also the voice of great poetry, of the Latin tradition, and, in the medieval mind, a prophet foretelling the coming of Christ. Dante's Virgil is thus a figure of awesome authority and it is he who initiates the journey:

> Ond' io per lo tuo me' penso e discerno
> che tu mi segui, e io sarò tua guida,
> e trarrotti di qui per loco etterno;
>   ove udirai le disperate strida,
> vedrai li antichi spiriti dolenti,
> cha' la seconda morte ciascun grida;
>   e vederai color che son contenti
> nel foco, perché speran di venire
> quando che sia a le beate genti.

> Therefore, considering what is best for you,
> I judge you should follow me. I shall be your guide
> to lead you through an eternal place where you shall
> hear the despairing shrieks of ancient spirits in pain
> who each bewail their second death. Then you shall
> see those who are content in the fire since they hope
> to come, whenever that shall be, among the blessed souls.

They begin their descent, Dante afraid of the prospect but Virgil certain that in the end his pupil will glimpse beatitude. The two men pass through the gates of Hell. Once through these, they hear the loud lamentations that resound through the starless air. The suggestion of myriads of souls is powerfully enforced. These are the wretched who lived without blame or praise, the morally neutral who, never more than half alive, have no hope of death. Incapable even of the grandeur of sin (one is inevitably reminded of Baudelaire, see pp. 112–13), they follow a wavering banner, the symbol of their moral rootlessness. Behind the leaders follow so great a train of people that

> ... ch'i' non averei creduto
> che morte tanta n'avesse disfatta.

> I had not thought that death had undone so many.

Such souls whirl naked through the outworks of Hell, stung by wasps and hornets, while the blood and tears that stream down their faces are gathered at their feet by loathsome worms.

When Dante has recovered from a faint, the two poets descend into the first of the series of concentric circles of Hell that become progressively narrower on their way to Satan's pit. Here, in the first circle, Dante encounters the virtuous heathen: great souls, sinless and not without merit, who nonetheless died before the time of Christ and so, since they were not baptized, could not worship God in the proper Christian way. Virgil himself is one of this number who live hopelessly in Hell, wracked with desire for salvation. They lament not as the worthless do, but sigh in untormented grief. It is to such as these that Eliot refers us when he describes the 'sighs, short and infrequent' that his London commuters make. Eliot sees these modern people, the businessmen and secretaries flooding into London, as the huge waste of the morally worthless or, at best, those whose vision – however worthy – cannot lift them above the level of human values. They may be good, but, having no real contact with salvation, they are condemned to spiritual sterility (see pp. 51–2). By describing the modern world through the language and associations of a past time rich in spiritual insight, Eliot here shows perfectly his technique of analysing the present through contact with tradition.

A further reference to *Inferno* comes at the close of the poem where Eliot is discussing the virtue of sympathy (ll. 410–16). He uses the story of Count Ugolino, which comes from near the end of *Inferno* and is a tale whose unspeakable nastiness has always been one of the poem's chief delights. Dante is now in those circles of Hell where treachery is punished. In this region of ice he encounters two men frozen in a single hole, the one stretched over the other's head like a hood and gnawing at his skull. They

are Count Ugolino and Archbishop Ruggieri. Both were treacherous.
Ugolino was a leading Pisan nobleman who, in the struggle between the
Guelph and Ghibelline factions in the political struggles that split
fourteenth-century Italy, changed sides to suit his own advantage. The
precise details need not concern us beyond knowing that Ugolino was first
opposed to the archbishop and then joined forces with him against his
own allies. In his turn, the archbishop broke with Ugolino and turned the
people against him. So much is squalid petty politics. It was the archbishop's revenge that is so singularly revolting. He imprisoned Ugolino and
four of his relations – Dante here makes them his sons – in a tower, nailed
up the door and, as Ugolino had foreseen in a dream, starved them all
to death. The simple concreteness of Dante's language is horribly effective:

> e io senti' chiavar l'uscio di sotto
> a l'orribile torre; ond' io guardai
> nel viso a' mie' figliuoi sanza far motto.
> Io non piangëa, sì dentro impetrai:
> piangevan elli; . . .

> and I heard below the door
> of the dreadful tower nailed up, and I looked
> at the faces of my sons without a word.
> I did not weep, I had so turned to stone within.
> They wept . . .

The children slowly die. Only the moon, passing across a little chink,
tells of the progress of time as the father, left alone and blind from
starvation, gropes over the corpses of his children.

It is to the nailing up of the door that Eliot refers us in his note to
ll. 411–12, and it is the horrors of solitary death that this reference is
supposed to trigger. But there is more than this. The *Inferno* is not a
waxworks horror show. Ugolino's fate is so terrible that sheer pity forces
us to forgive him. Why, then, is he being punished? Why is he in Hell, his
thwarted paternal affections perverted to terrible and eternal revenge?
The answer lies in his own treachery, which, however dreadfully punished
on earth, is yet, particularly for Dante, a sin of enormous consequence.
The cold-blooded traitor seeking his own advantage is the most antisocial
of sinners, the destroyer of the social order which – at least in its ideal form
– was for Dante the work of God. To abuse it was a deadly offence. It
locks a man in a purely private universe in which he seeks only his own
advantage. There is no sympathy here, no working for the commonweal.
One form of spiritual death, Eliot is saying, is total and sterile selfishness.
In political terms, this means the self-seeking individualism of Ugolino
and Coriolanus (see p.138).

The last reference to Dante which we should discuss comes in that complex and desperate web of quotation at the close of the poem (see p. 48). Here, in the image of Arnaut Daniel slipping back into the refining fire (l. 427), we are in the world of the *Purgatorio* and possible salvation.

If the *Inferno* is a place of horror in which – according to the standards of Christian justice – men must suffer eternal punishment for finite sins, then the *Purgatorio* presents a more ordered world of expiation which Dante shares as he winds his way around its Mountain of the Seven Deadly Sins. When, he, too, has passed through the refining fire, he is prepared for the next stage of his journey, the vision of heaven and

> pura luce:
> luce intellettual, piena d'amore;
> amor di vero ben pien di letizia.

> pure light;
> intellectual light full of love,
> love of true good, full of happiness.

It is intellectual light and love such as this, the combination of the beatitude and joy found in faith, that is the final end. And it is with the relation of human to divine love that the *Purgatorio* is much concerned. This had always been a prime concern of Dante's and it is reflected in his meeting with Arnaut Daniel.

Dante's earliest poetry is important and valuable in its own right. He introduced into it the conventions of courtly love of refined spiritualized longing and agonized despair that were Europe's inheritance from the troubadours of Provence. Translated into Italian, it became the *dolce stil nuovo* ('sweet new style') as Dante calls it.

Of the two masters from whom he learnt that such love is overpowering and irrational, one, Guido Guinizelli, he meets here first. This was the man whose work Dante developed. By a series of huge imaginative leaps, he progressed far beyond Guinizelli's idea of love the destroyer of intellect and virtue, and came to see it as a choice made by reason and will. It was rational and purifying, and it was because of this that Beatrice – Dante's dead mistress – can embody such ideas and lead him from Purgatory into Heaven and the sight of God whose love can 'move the sun and other stars'.

It is particularly appropriate that near the close of the *Purgatorio*, in the circle of the repenting lustful and just before he encounters Beatrice, Dante should meet his old poetic mentors, Guinizelli in particular. He is shown moving hopefully in the refining fire because of his 'good sorrowing' before his end. He had come close to repentance. Once the poet of irrational, destructive passion, he is now aware of love's redemptive power. Dante talks to him as a fellow poet, and at the close of their conversation he sees another spirit, the Provençal Arnaut Daniel, a 'miglior fabbro', a better craftsman than Guinizelli (this, of course, is the epithet that Eliot applied to Ezra Pound, his own mentor: see pp. 30 and 31). And it is Arnaut Daniel who provides Eliot with his reference. Here is the poet who – in Dante's opinion – purified the dialect of his people to make it a medium of ideas that Guinizelli would take over and Dante greatly expand. He allows Arnaut Daniel to talk here in his own Provençal and has him describe himself as one who weeps and sings as he goes in the fire. Daniel sees his past follies with grief and rejoices in the hope of future deliverance. He asks Dante to pray for him: 'Ara vos prec.' Then he 'hides himself in the fire that refines them', as we may translate Eliot's quotation of:

Poi s'ascose nel foco chegli affina.

In a sense, this is one of the most hopeful of the allusions at the close of *The Waste Land.* Certainly, it relates to many of the poem's themes. The lust of St. Augustine in Carthage is seen as a form of burning (see pp. 127–9), while the 'Fire Sermon' of the Buddha presents unenlightened men burning in the flames of their senses (see pp. 119–20). We have seen also that throughout the poem sexuality has been debased into lust and neurosis. Sexual inadequacy characterizes both the house agent's clerk and the hostile woman in 'A Game of Chess'. Here, very briefly, is the possibility of something else. In the circle of the lustful in the *Purgatorio,* fire – a symbol of their sin – is also the hope of something beyond sin: purgation dependent on a complete faith in God's final justice.

At the close of *The Waste Land,* then, is a glimpse of purgatory. Throughout the poem Dante has provided Eliot with some of his most coherent symbols of spiritual distress. From the enormous confidence and range of the *Divine Comedy* Eliot selected those moments which could act as triggers, moments by which the modern world could be measured against a richer and far different one. Here, in Dante, was a poet whose spiritual pilgrimage was to provide Eliot with a lifetime's resources. Dante wrote out of the heart of Christian certainty. For him, the journey through Hell was a prelude to the discovery of Heaven. This was explicit from the start. The same was not yet true of Eliot. God and Heaven do not define the Hell of *The Waste Land.* It is a wholly secular place and it is the sterility of the secular which accounts for its anguish. Such suffering as this is not a prelude to any religious certainties. It bears no relation to divine justice. Arnaut Daniel retreating into the purgatorial fire is a very brief view of the remote possibility opened up by the experience of others: that the lustful sexuality of *The Waste Land* may one day be redeemed.

Buddhism

> *What we are today comes from our thoughts of yesterday, and our present thoughts build our life of tomorrow: our life is the creation of our mind.*
>
> *If a man speaks or acts with an impure mind, suffering follows him as the wheel of the cart follows the beast that draws the cart.*
>
> Dhammapada (*trans. Juan Mascaro*)

Eliot took the title of one of the Buddha's sermons for the title of the third section of *The Waste Land*. At the close of this he fuses its subject matter with reminiscences of St. Augustine's *Confessions* and comments: 'The collocation of these two representatives of eastern and western asceticism, as the culmination of this part of the poem, is not an accident.' We should therefore try to trace the importance of *The Fire Sermon* in Buddhist teaching.

At the heart of Buddhism lies the enlightenment of the Buddha himself. Born a prince and sheltered from knowledge of the world's ills, the inevitable contact with age, illness and death roused in him an irresistible desire to find the causes of suffering and their solution. To this end, he gave up the life of his palace and for six years meditated on the problem of pain, imposing on himself the greatest physical austerity. Despite such discipline he found no answer. Eventually, at the age of thirty-five, he seated himself under a tree in the lotus position of meditation and vowed not to rise until he had achieved enlightenment. After a night of profound spiritual experience, he rose the next day as the All-Enlightened One.

Suffering and freedom from suffering lie at the heart of the Buddhist vision, and the cause of suffering is selfish desire. Each person sees himself as separate, unique, individual, and this self is the centre of his interest. How he wishes to exploit it may vary. A man may long to do good works or he may be consumed with lust. Either path is his karma, the destiny that he has created for himself by the things he has yearned to do: 'What we are today comes from our thoughts of yesterday.' Desiring to act on the world weaves man into a net of cause and effect, and this binds him tight. As the English Buddhist Christmas Humphries has commented:

... Even as the causes generated by one man react upon that man, so the mass causation of a group, be it family, society or nation, reacts upon that group as such, and upon all whose karma places them at the time they are in. Each man has, therefore, several 'karmas', racial, national, family and personal, yet all quite properly *his*, else he would not have found himself subject to their sway.

Man is caught on the wheel, the endless revolution of cause and effect, because he believes in the power of his separate, illusory self which wants now this, now that, now another thing. But this lower self is an illusion precisely because it is changed by its various wants. It is never the same but is in a constant state of flux. Such flux is suffering:

Birth is suffering, decay is suffering, disease is suffering, death is suffering, association with the unpleasing is suffering, separation from the pleasing is suffering, not to get what one wants is suffering.

The way beyond suffering is to realize that the self to which we are so attached has no fixed reality. Man must get beyond the circumstances that cause desire: 'Our mind should stand aloof from circumstances, and on no account should we allow them to influence the function of our minds.' We must go beyond karma and free ourselves from the Wheel of Life by right action and thought – what is known in Buddhism as the Noble Eightfold path and which includes such characteristic activities as meditation – and so enter nirvana, that state described as coming to pass when, after 'the destruction of all that is individual in us, we enter into communion with the whole universe and become an integral part of the great purpose'.

Such freedom from desire – particularly sterile sexual desire – is one clear way out of *The Waste Land.* However, just as in his use of Dante Eliot could refer only to the world of the *Inferno* and *Purgatorio,* so with Buddhism it is not the final beatific end that is glimpsed in *The Waste Land;* rather, it is the analysis of worldly suffering provided by religious experience. This is particularly clear in Eliot's citing of *The Fire Sermon.* This was actually preached to a group of Indian fire-worshippers whose beliefs formed its imagery. In the sermon, Buddha describes how burning desire binds men to the world and to illusion and suffering. Freedom from these is the goal of the wise man:

All things are on fire; the eye is on fire, forms are on fire, eye-consciousness is on fire; the impressions received by the eye are on fire, and whatever sensation originates in the impressions received by the eye is likewise on fire. And with what are these things on fire? With the fires of lust, anger and illusion, with these they are on fire, and so were the other senses and so was the mind. Wherefore the wise man conceives disgust for the things of the senses, and being divested of desire for the things of the senses, he removes from his heart the cause of suffering.

In *The Waste Land* the Narrator still feels consumed with desire, and in this he is at one with St. Augustine wracked by the lust of Carthage. The two make a 'collocation' here because their experience of the Waste Land of lust and desire is similar. So, too, was their belief that the solution to the problem was ascetic and spiritual.

The *Upanishads*

> *In the whole of the world there is no study so beneficial and so elevating as that of the* Upanishads. *It has been the solace of my life – it will be the solace of my death.*

> *Schopenhauer*

Near the end of *The Waste Land*, after the disappointment of the empty Grail chapel, the Narrator sees a flash of lightning and feels the promise of rain. We return to the vegetation cults, the rites that secured the fertility of the land (see pp. 94–9), but we also move forward to the Hindu teachings of the *Upanishads*.

At the core of these Sanskrit gospels (which date from about 600 B.C.) is the idea that the goal of man's religious quest lies in identifying his self, or *atman*, with *brahman*, the supreme source of all things. It is a mystical union in which the ego frees itself and the soul is at one with the great cosmic force who fashioned the world out of his self-delighting creativity. The core of the individual is now joined to the essence of the universe. It is a state of heightened sense of being, consciousness and delight. The spirit of this is well expressed in a section from the *Chandogya Upanishad*:

All this universe is in truth brahman. He is the beginning and end and life of all. As such, in silence, give unto him adoration.

Man in truth is made of faith. As his faith is in this life, so he becomes in the beyond: with faith and vision let him work.

There is a Spirit that is in mind and life, light and truth and vast spaces. He contains all works and desires and all perfumes and all tastes. He enfolds the whole universe, and in silence is loving to all.

This is the Spirit that is in my heart, smaller than a grain of rice, or a grain of barley, or a grain of mustard-seed, or a grain of canary-seed, or the kernel of a grain of canary-seed. This is the Spirit that is in my heart, greater than the earth, greater than the sky, greater than heaven itself, greater than all these worlds.

He contains all works and desires and all perfumes and all tastes. He enfolds the whole universe and in silence is loving to all. This is the Spirit that is in my heart, this is brahman.

To him I shall come when I go beyond this life. And to him will come he who has faith and doubts not.

(trans. Juan Mascaró)

The sense of peace and awe is very strong here. The supreme is manifest in every soul. Hinduism teaches that the union between the self and the supreme source of life may be made in many ways: through work, meditation, knowledge, devotion. But man is 'made of faith', and as is his faith, so is his life. If he gives himself over to selfish pursuits, then he binds himself to suffering, illusion and endless cycles of rebirth. There are clear analogies to Buddhism here, as indeed there are in the idea that it is through preserving the correct forms of behaviour that a man preserves his vision of the infinite. Our suffering comes from selfishness, which is a form of ignorance. The self, however, is an illusion when seen as something separate from God. Hinduism therefore emphasizes a moral code and practice which guides men away from selfish ignorance and back to their true end. Such 'right action' is brought out in the section from the parable in the *Brihadaranyaka Upanishad* which Eliot quotes at the close of the poem.

The parable tells how when the gods, men and the devils had finished their student days with Pragapati, the Lord of Creation, they asked him for some final words of wisdom. To each he uttered the syllable *'Da'*. The gods understood this to have been *'Damyata'*, meaning 'to be subdued' or 'self-controlled' (this is not, it would appear, Eliot's understanding of the term, see p. 47). Men thought he said *'Datta'*, which is the Sanskrit for 'give'; while the evil spirits thought they heard him say *'Dayadhvan'*, or 'be merciful'.

The presentation here of the Lord of Creation as a god calls for some explanation. After all, the passages from the *Upanishads* make it clear that he is a force rather than an incarnate deity. In fact, Hinduism recognizes the supreme difficulty of visualizing a purely spiritual godhead and so allows incarnation in many forms as an aid to worship. In this particular case, the incarnation of the source of life as Indra, a deity who could take on an endless variety of forms at will, is important since he is the god who, with his thunderbolt in his right hand, is the dispenser of thunder and lightning. Indra is the god of rain and fertility who is constantly at war with drought.

It is this figure who thus brings to a head the vegetation gods who have their roles in the earlier sections of the poem. Indra, the God of Thunder, suggests the promise of a Waste Land redeemed through rain. But he is more than this. He comes in the lightning, and lightning is an Indian symbol of enlightenment. The enlightenment that he brings is the moral teaching of the *Brihadaranyaka Upanishad*:

> The divine voice of thunder repeats the same Da Da Da, that is, Be subdued, Give, Be merciful. Therefore let that triad be taught, Subduing, Giving, Mercy.

Here are the Hindu principles of 'right action', whose practice has little to do with the intellect and nothing to do with selfish desire. They are a form of moral teaching that also happen to be associated with fertility. They do not in themselves bring rain, but, in Eliot's interpretation, they are close to some of the Narrator's most spiritual experiences (ll. 395–422), which are in turn connected with the possibility of a Waste Land redeemed. It is partly for this reason that Eliot can end his poem with the three repeated Sanskrit words that close an *Upanishad* and mean in a western, Christianized translation: 'The Peace which passeth all understanding'.

Hermann Hesse

'In Sight of Chaos'

Title of an essay by Hermann Hesse

The fear that underlies *The Waste Land* is not a purely personal neurosis. Much of the work's power comes from its sense of a whole history and culture collapsing from fatigue, futility and impotence. This sense of a world in chaos is powerfully expressed in a section from 'What The Thunder said':

> What is that sound high in the air
> Murmur of maternal lamentation
> Who are those hooded hordes swarming
> Over endless plains, stumbling in cracked earth
> Ringed by the flat horizon only

The passage ends with an apocalyptic vision of the fall of the great western cities. In his Notes to these lines, Eliot refers us to Hermann Hesse's essay *Blick ins Chaos* ('In Sight of Chaos'), from which he then quotes the last line.

Hesse's work is a study of Dostoevsky's *The Brothers Karamazov*, or, more precisely, a meditation on how the insights of that work, in Hesse's view, prefigure the collapse of Europe. For Hesse, traditional Europe was tired. Taking a psychological model of its culture, he sees the maintenance of civilization as a conflict between man's higher faculties and his unconscious, a conflict which has now resulted in exhaustion:

> Man, half-way between animal and a higher consciousness, has always a great deal within him to repress, to hide, to deny, in order to be a decent human being and to be socially possible. Man is full of animal, full of primeval being, full of the tremendous, scarcely tamed instincts of a beastly, cruel selfishness. All these dangerous instincts are there always. But culture, super-consciousness, civilization, have covered them over. Man does not show them, he has learnt from childhood to hide these instincts and to deny them. But every one of these instincts must come sooner or later to the surface.

It is precisely these instincts that Hesse now sees emerging as a result of the decay and fatigue of western culture. The reason for that decay and tiredness was a failure of nerve, and 'to have bad nerves is the colloquial term for hysteria and neurasthenia, for moral insanity . . .' Such neurosis as this is so clearly an aspect of *The Waste Land* that it will be interesting to see how Hesse develops his ideas.

That neurosis was destructive, Hesse was not in doubt. There were, however, two possible responses. The first, reserved for what he calls 'the Knights of a treasured morality', will be to mourn inconsolably for the passing of ways of disciplined thought that had their origin in Greek democracy and Roman law and found their greatest modern fulfilment in empirical science. For the rest – the visionaries – the decay is a prelude to an exciting new birth.

For Hesse, this process of decay followed by rebirth was like the period of adolescence. As the culture in which men live becomes exhausted, so the people themselves become more remarkable. They become hysterical, develop strange lusts and longings 'for which man has no name'. The period of collapse is thus also a period of anarchic spiritual experiment, and Hesse associates this with a longing for the east, for Russia and for what he analyses as the 'Karamazov type'. This is the man who (bringing together all the characteristics of the brothers in Dostoevsky's novel) is at once hysterical, drunken, a felon, poet and saint. He is a spiritual voyager defying bourgeois values, an impulsive, contradictory blend of cruelty and self-sacrifice, but a man who in his new liberation is, in the deepest sense, an innocent. Above all, such people are 'constantly concerned with their souls'. They live deeply in their imaginations, and for them the possibility of a crime or a good deed – the mere imagining of it – is of crucial significance, for what has only been imagined is never forgotten. It becomes part of mankind's spiritual repertoire.

In Hesse's opinion, Europe was now longing for this liberation into a new consciousness. He believed Europe to be tired and wanting to turn 'homewards':

The ideal of the Karamazov, primeval, Asiatic and occult, is already beginning to consume the European soul. This is what I mean by the downfall of Europe. This downfall is a return home to the mother, a turning back to Asia, to the source ... and will necessarily lead, like every death of earth, to a new birth.

Hesse himself did not see this process – as Eliot was more prone to (see p. 14) – as physical revolution. For him, it was possible that it would play itself out inwardly 'in the souls of a generation ... in changing the meaning of worn-out symbols, in the dis-valuation of spiritual values'.

This clearly brings us close to *The Waste Land*, but Hesse's essay is not a simple blueprint for Eliot's poem. Hesse was wholly optimistic about the change he foresaw. For him, the hope of regeneration, however distant, was worth all the threats of moral anarchy. For Kaiser Wilhelm II, such anarchy was a more pressing worry, defined by Hesse as 'a vague fear of the eastern hordes, which ... might be enrolled against Europe'. This is close to Eliot's position too. It is suggested in the lines from 'What the Thunder said' that we have already quoted. Anarchy terrified him, and if he recognized that the spiritual had indeed become a drunken man, there was little in hysteria itself which caused Eliot to rejoice. Of course, he had recognized the great spiritual value of eastern religions. This is clear in his use of the *Upanishads*, but this did not mean that Eliot welcomed Hesse's view of chaos. Shoring up his fragments against his ruins, Eliot is closer to Hesse's 'Knights of a treasured morality' in his view of Europe. He sees Europe, in the words of Hesse that he quotes, as being:

In a state of drunken illusion ... reeling into the abyss and, as she reels, [singing] a drunken hymn such as Dmitri Karamazov sang. The insulted citizen laughs that song to scorn, the Saint and Seer hear it with tears.

Richard Wagner

Tristan und Isolde is one of the world's supreme expressions of romantic love: a torrent of fatal passion, sexuality and death. The musical motifs that wind their way through it are of an extraordinary intensity, but they are brought to their climax only at the moment of death in Isolde's famous *Liebestod* (song of love and death). The precise details of the opera's plot are unimportant to us here. What does matter is the atmosphere for which the quotations that Eliot uses provide a trigger: feelings of hatred and vengeance turned to a miraculous love that floats in its amoral beauty above all social constraints, but is, at the same time, allied to death and the idea that for Isolde (as for Wagner) Desire is 'the gateway to Death, and Death the sublimation of Desire'. Faintly, and against Eliot's main theme of sterility and decay, we hear through his quotations (ll. 31–4 and 42) the expression of this grand and tragic theme.

The first Act of *Tristan und Isolde* takes place on the boat in which Tristan is taking Isolde from Ireland to marry his uncle in Cornwall. The relation of passion to the sea is strong in Wagner and it is also, of course, a guiding image in *The Waste Land* (see pp. 71–5). As the opera opens, Isolde is lying distraught in her tapestry-hung apartment on the foredeck. The voice of a young sailor introduces the scene with a charming song:

> The wind so wild blows homeward now:
> My Irish child, where tarriest thou?

To the reader who knows Wagner opera, Eliot's quotations suggest immediately a lyrical melancholy soon to be swept up in torrents of anguish. They may also suggest the other images of sailing in Eliot's poem (ll. 418–22), but the return to *'oed' und leer das Meer'* ('open and desolate the sea') will remind him of the dying Tristan as he waits for Isolde, her love and redeeming powers, in a set which Wagner describes as a castle in a garden by the sea: 'The whole suggests the absence of a master, ill kept, and here and there ... dilapidated and overgrown.' Here is a Waste Land of failed passion, and Tristan lies dying here of his wound, just like the Fisher King. The lovers, however, can only be finally united in death – Isolde cannot save Tristan for this world – and in the musical and dramatic climax of the work – the *Liebestod* – she sinks beneath the waves of Tristan's breath, which grow in her mind to a cosmic delirium of death and longing:

> In the swell of their surge, in their clamorous tone,
> In the vast wave breath of the world
> To drown, to sink, unaware,
> Highest bliss!

The other image that Wagner offered Eliot also concerned water and the idea of the subaqueous world. This was the gold once hoarded by the Rhinemaidens but stolen from them and made into the magic Ring around the possession of which are based Wagner's four vast music dramas of *Der Ring des Nibelungen*. Eliot alludes to the last part of this work, *The Twilight of the Gods*, and to the Chorus of the Rhinemaidens which opens its final Act, in the lyrical section in 'The Fire Sermon' (ll. 266–99). Here, the Thames, seen simultaneously in its contemporary and Elizabethan life, offers first a melancholy beauty offset by its pollution, then an overwrought passage of feckless love reminiscent of the opening to 'A Game of Chess' (ll. 279–91), and is finally associated with the desperate ending of love and the meaninglessness of all existence.

In *The Twilight of the Gods*, the Rhinemaidens similarly associate the theft of their gold with the darkness and joylessness of their river. The Ring that has been made from their treasure is cursed, associated with destruction, betrayal and the loss of love. At the end of the opera, the golden Ring will indeed be returned to them. It will have wrought its havoc on man and the gods and will be taken back to where

> The flood alone
> Its curse can allay.

Once again, images of water purge the Waste Land.

St. Augustine

> *... he possessed a strong, capacious, argumentative mind; he boldly sounded the dark abyss of grace, predestination, free-will, and original sin; and the rigid system of Christianity which he framed or restored has been entertained with public applause and secret reluctance by the Latin Church.*
>
> *Edward Gibbon,* The Decline and Fall of the Roman Empire

St. Augustine is one of the great figures of early Christianity, and his *Confessions* are the first European example of true autobiographical writing. St. Augustine appears only briefly in *The Waste Land*, but he is placed significantly at the close of 'The Fire Sermon' alongside the Buddha as the exponent of western 'asceticism'.

St. Augustine was born into the collapsing world of classical culture. He was fifty-six when Alaric sacked Rome in 410 A.D. This background is of importance, particularly in the context of *The Waste Land*, for the *Confessions* set Augustine's struggle towards Christian faith and certainty in the context of a decaying world, of what he later came to regard as the false intellectual standards of paganism and, more immediately to our purpose, the restless sexuality of Carthage. We have here a further example of a man depicting his spiritual and emotional bankruptcy – his private Waste Land – in a great city.

'Thou madest us for thyself, O Lord, and our hearts are restless till they rest in thee.' These lines from the opening of the *Confessions* are a clear indication of the book's theme: St. Augustine's progress towards God during the first thirty-two years of his life. He was born into a relatively modest home, but both his father and his mother – the latter's conversion to Christianity and deep piety Augustine delightfully records – wished for him to improve himself. In the late classical world this meant studying rhetoric. To this end, at the age of sixteen or so, Augustine was sent to Carthage. He was already deeply in the toils of adolescence, and the retrospective view of the *Confessions* shows us a man who had proudly exalted in his free will and sexual and intellectual prowess, only to find that these things finally led him to the Church. In this passage, which is the one to which Eliot refers (ll. 307–11), there is a convincing picture of a sexually aware teenager desperate for love and adventure:

I went to Carthage, where I found myself in the midst of a hissing cauldron of lust. I had not yet fallen in love, but I was in love with the idea of it, and this feeling that something was missing made me despise myself for not being more anxious to satisfy the need. I began to look around for some object for my love, since I badly wanted to love something. I had no liking for the safe path without pitfalls, for although my real need was for you, my God, who are the food of the soul, I was not aware of this hunger. I felt no need for the food that does not perish, not because I had had my fill of it, but because the more I was starved of it the less palatable it seemed. Because of this my soul fell sick. It broke out in ulcers and looked about desperately for some material, worldly means of relieving the itch which they caused. But material things, which have no soul, could not be true objects for my love. To love and to have my love returned was my heart's desire, and it would be all the sweeter if I could also enjoy the body of the one who loved me.

So I muddied the stream of friendship with the filth of lewdness and clouded its clear waters with hell's black river of lust. And yet, in spite of this rank depravity, I was vain enough to have ambitions of cutting a fine figure in the world. I also fell in love, which was a snare of my own choosing. My God, my God of mercy, how good you were to me, for you mixed much bitterness in that cup of pleasure! My love was returned and finally shackled me in the bonds of its consummation. In the midst of my joy I was caught up in the coils of trouble, for I was lashed with the cruel, fiery rods of jealousy and suspicion, fear, anger, and quarrels.

(trans. R. S. Pine-Coffin)

Carthage thus became an inferno. The restraints and sense of order which the earlier classical world had enjoyed were no longer powerful. Civilization as it had been known was in a state of collapse. To the young, there remained the possibilities of professional ambition – and Augustine was a very ambitious man – and sex. In the *Confessions*, the intellectual is finally the more important. Augustine's ambition was far from simply acquiring the money he would earn by the exercise of his skills; rather, his love of philosophy and the pursuit of truth led him to embrace and then dismiss the various systems of thought his day offered him until he came to a full acceptance of a Christianity shorn of contemporary heresies.

This struggle is less the issue in reference to *The Waste Land* than St. Augustine's fight with what he presents as his powerful sexual drive. This, indulged for its own sake and outside the Christian constraints of marriage, failed to prove his final emotional resting place.

Throughout his autobiography Augustine presents his life in such a way that we are made to feel the purpose of God working in it and bringing the sinner through grief and humbled pride back to Himself. Hence the shrewd analysis of sexual misery. St. Augustine shows that sex is not a sufficient end, that it corrupts into a restless and deeply painful lust; while the need for love, though it can be answered by another human being, is not really complete until that person is loved as a fellow child of God rather than for his or her own sake. In his teens and early twenties Augustine was hardly aware of this, but, in retrospect, the emotional and sexual sufferings of his early manhood could be seen as the anguish of the soul without God, the restlessness of a heart without faith.

It is this burning in lust and restlessness that Eliot compares to the enlightened Buddha's view of men wholly subject to natural appetites (see pp. 119–20), but, as with all of Eliot's more effective allusions, the inclusion of St. Augustine at the climax of 'The Fire Sermon' may be felt through the whole poem. The presence of St. Augustine (and hence of a deep-seated sexual unhappiness in a civilization collapsing through the lack of spiritual resources) enriches *The Waste Land* considerably. It is a further example of the unity of emotional and cultural health and of how the collapse of the one is mirrored in the decline of the other.

Latin writers and the poets of *The Greek Anthology*

> 'Oh, Oenothea, it's this young man you see here,' she said, 'he was born under an evil star. He can't make a sale to boy or girl. You've never seen a man so unlucky – he's got a piece of wet leather, not a penis.'
>
> *Petronius,* Satyricon (*trans. J. P. Sullivan*)

The most important classical figures to influence *The Waste Land* are the writers who created the character of Tiresias: Sophocles, Seneca and Ovid (see pp. 107–9). However, four Latin works contributed further references to the poem; the *Satyricon* of Petronius, the anonymous *Pervigilium Veneris*, the section from Ovid's *Metamorphoses* which tells the tale of Philomela and, lastly, the *Aeneid* of Virgil. To these we may add the poets of *The Greek Anthology*.

Satyricon – the Cumaean Sybil

The *Satyricon* is the brilliant but fragmentary prose epic of the unofficial 'arbiter of elegance' to the court of the Emperor Nero. In so far as its narrative thread can be reconstructed, it tells of the adventures of Encolpius and his sixteen-year-old boyfriend. There is much tenderness in the work, particularly in the relationship between Encolpius and Giton, but by far the greatest portion of the work is satirical. The form seems to be mock epic: in other words, a comic inversion of the great poems of antiquity, in this case Homer's *Odyssey*. In the earlier work, Odysseus is pursued by the vengeful Poseidon; in the *Satyricon*, in a way that is not wholly clear, Encolpius has profaned the rites of the Roman fertility god Priapus and is impotent as a result. He, Giton and the various other figures whom they meet move through a world racked by elegantly described depravity: a world of the new and vulgarly rich, of bad poets, predatory women and bizarre adventure. Perhaps the most famous remaining scene, and certainly the one where Petronius's eye for visual detail and ear for colloquial speech are strongest, is the banquet of Trimalchio, the self-made millionaire. It is he who, during the course of a gargantuan meal and just before the description of his lavish tomb, tells the story of the Cumaean Sybil which provided Eliot with his epigraph (see pp. 30–31). Trimalchio is at this point boring his dinner guests with old stories and spoof learning:

'In fact I actually saw the Sybil at Cumae with my own eyes dangling in a bottle, and when the children asked her in Greek: "What do you want Sybil?" she used to answer: "I want to die."'

The Cumaean Sybil, who had been Aeneas's guide to the underworld, was one of the famous soothsayers of antiquity. Like her sisters, she was regarded as being immortal but as not having the gift of eternal youth. She is thus in some respects like Tiresias: an ancient prophet who brings no hope of salvation. Rather, a tired relic of the past, she hangs ignominiously in her bottle, judged by the vulgar present and wishing only to die.

Beyond the epigraph it is difficult to say how much Petronius suggested to Eliot. The idea of impotence is clearly related to his poem. The fragmentary state of the work and its consequent violent juxtapositions and moral tone may also have helped. The sense of a civilization at its end is certainly similar. But perhaps its 'mixed' style, the interweaving of rhetoric and colloquial speech (compare 'A Game of Chess'), the sense of parody and allusion, were also useful.

Pervigilium Veneris – *'Quando fiam uti chelidon'*

The *Pervigilium Veneris* ('The Vigil of Venus') provided Eliot with one fragment for the close of *The Waste Land: Quando fiam uti chelidon* ('When shall I be as the swallow?'). Taken out of context, it expresses a certain longing for freedom; but if we place it in relation to the whole of that lovely, very late Latin poem, then a greater richness of reference is clear.

The poem evokes the religious celebration of Venus Genetrix: the goddess of love in her role as the principle of sexual reproduction. We are again in the world of ancient fertility cults. A lovely aura of expectancy of spring, rain and thriving plants, youth, love and the health of the Roman state suffuses all but the last verse. Such spring-like innocence and well-being are the very opposite to *The Waste Land*. But in the last quatrain there is an ancient melancholy. The anonymous poet asks when his own spring will come, when, like the swallow, will he be given a voice with which to sing. His inspiration is now dead and the poet perishes in his silence. He and, by analogy, the Narrator of *The*

Waste Land have been cut off from love and healthy fertility, cut off too from the well-being of the state. Sterile dissatisfaction destroys their craft. In its context, the quotation could not be more just.

The Rape of Philomel

The boudoir in the opening lines of 'A Game of Chess' contains a *trompe-l'œil* painting of 'the change of Philomel'. This is a further sample of the cruelty of Greek myth (especially in sexual matters) that so distressed Eliot.

The story is briefly told. King Tereus married Procne, the daughter of the ruler of Athens. He then fell in love with her sister, Philomela, and so locked Procne away in the slaves' quarters and let it be known that she was dead. While escorting Philomela to her marriage in his kingdom, Tereus raped her and then cut out her tongue to prevent her telling. The outraged sister managed to communicate with Procne, and she, in her mute fury, slew the son she had had by Tereus, gutted him and then boiled him for Tereus to eat. When Tereus realized he was eating the flesh of his own son, he pursued the vengeful sisters as they fled from his palace and was about to murder them both when the gods transformed Procne into a swallow, Philomela into a nightingale and Tereus into a hoopoe. The nightingale, of course, is a conventional part of pastoral verse, its voice the song of love. However, the refrain 'Jug jug' is also Elizabethan slang for sexual intercourse, and, by quoting it in the context of the myth, Eliot is able to hint at a romantic pastoral, its debasement into the merely physical, and the savagery of rape and murder from which the whole idea springs. This combination of violence and the debasement of love is particularly appropriate to *The Waste Land*.

Virgil

The reference to Virgil in 'A Game of Chess' is a passing one. The 'laquearia' or panelled ceiling of the boudoir comes from the first book of the *Aeneid* where Dido, Queen of Carthage, is sumptuously entertaining the hero, her lover. Eventually, of course, she is deserted by him. The call of Fate, the mission to found Rome, is of greater importance than the love of this woman. The deserted Dido commits suicide, and the tragic love-affair provides an ironic background to the fragmenting relationship we are watching here.

The Greek Anthology

The Greek Anthology is a collection of over four thousand epigrams on a very wide range of subjects. A few of them are epitaphs for those drowned at sea. Pound had long been attracted to them and had translated some. While the Phlebas episode is not a translation, it bears obvious analogies to such a poem as this with its terse pathos:

> Sudden strong squalls from the sou'-west
> Night, and the waves that dark Orion stirs
> At his November setting – these were my fate.
> And I, Callaeschrus, wrenched from life
> As I sailed the mid-Lybian waters, my bones
> Now thread the sea, as the fish and the tides turn them,
> And this stone lies that says it lies on me.
>
> *(trans. Clive Sanson)*

The Bible

> *... I will lay it waste; it shall not be pruned, nor digged; but there shall come up briars and thorns: I will also command the clouds that they rain no rain upon it.*
>
> *Isaiah, 5.6*

The lamentations of the Hebrew prophets – as translated in the Authorized Version of the Bible – provide the traditional language of doom. In Ecclesiastes, Isaiah, Jeremiah and Ezekiel, the backsliding of the Jewish people is castigated with a rhetoric of vicious destruction. The Jews are – among many other images – the vineyard that will be laid waste and returned to the parched desert. Similar passages are used in Eliot's poem both explicitly (ll. 20–23) and more generally (ll. 19–30 and 331–4) for their suggestion of the unrighteous weighed against imminent destruction. It was natural that they should be. The Old Testament Jews, living disinherited on the edges of the desert, often abandoned and even cursed by God, constantly under threat of attack and falling into moral chaos while they waited endlessly for the Messiah, are an obvious source of Waste Land imagery, a source the more potent for its familiarity and the association of destruction and infertility with sin.

The Old Testament Jews' destiny of waiting for a Redeemer is clearly analogous to the themes of *The Waste Land*. Old Testament history is essentially one of expectation, the preservation of the race until the coming of the Messiah and the return to the Promised Land. The latter, especially in the vision of Ezekiel, is a world of water and fertility, a dream of a Waste Land at once physical, cultural and spiritual, prosperous and redeemed:

And it shall come to pass, that every thing that liveth, which moveth, whithersoever the rivers shall come, shall live: and there shall be a very great multitude of fish, because these waters shall come thither: for they shall be healed; and every thing shall live whither the river cometh.

Such is the longed-for end. But more typical of the Old Testament prophets are such images as this from the second chapter of Isaiah, where the righteous man in the times of the ungodly is exhorted to 'enter into the rock, and hide thee in the dust, for fear of the Lord' (compare ll. 24–30). The prophet has a vision of the Day of Judgement and of tumbling towers and cities (compare ll. 371–5). The mountains, too, are often seen as a source of inspiration, but at other times they are places of contrition and even of spiritual failure: 'Truly in vain is salvation hoped for from the hills, and from the multitude of the mountains' (compare ll. 331–4). In Jeremiah, the absence of God is seen as a period of burning and lust, a time of broken cisterns and empty wells (compare l. 384). The specific references which Eliot points out in his notes are to Ezekiel addressed by God (l. 20), while the cricket of l. 23 and the cicada of l. 353 are borrowed from the vision of the end in Ecclesiastes:

Also when they shall be afraid of that which is high, and fears shall be in the way, and the almond tree shall flourish, and the grasshopper shall be a burden, and desire shall fail: because man goeth to his long home, and the mourners go about the streets ...

Such references to the prophets of the Old Testament serve to widen the cultural inclusiveness of the poem: the sense of a tradition of Waste Land imagery common to all our inheritance. They deepen especially the theme of blinded spiritual insight and an infertility which is at once physical but also much more. The particular strength of the Old Testament references, however, lies not in the fairly exact correspondence between their images of sterility and those of other systems of belief, but rather in the significance they have accumulated, the effect of their continuous re-use by so many writers to suggest sin and the imminent wrath of God about to descend because of the irreligion and moral feebleness of the Jews.

The power of these biblical allusions is also partly a matter of language. Biblical citation is probably the most immediately emotive of all Eliot's references, and, by employing it, he could bring into his poem what is for most people the most obvious example of voices from the past commenting on the impotence of the present. Through the emotion aroused by the Old Testament, Eliot could provide his poem with a ready-made set of responses which include sinfulness, turning from God, the penance urged by the visionary and, perhaps above all, the drama of spiritual doom.

The Old Testament presents a world without a Redeemer. In Christian theology the New Testament is its fulfilment. Christ is the risen God who has triumphed over man's sin and won forgiveness for him. We have already seen the similarities between this belief and the fertility cults analysed by Frazer (see pp. 94–9), but in 'What the Thunder said' we are reminded of scenes in Christ's life immediately before the crucifixion (ll. 322–6) and after the resurrection (ll. 359–65); in other words, of Christ as man and of Christ as the resurrected Son of God.

The opening paragraph of 'What the Thunder said' has clear analogies and references to the period of Christ's arrest: the garden of Gethsemane, the soldiers and the imprisonment before the trial; but the latter passage (ll. 359–65) deals with the appearance of the resurrected Christ to his disciples on the road to Emmaus:

> Who is the third who walks always beside you?
> When I count, there are only you and I together
> But when I look ahead up the white road
> There is always another one walking beside you
> Gliding wrapt in a brown mantle, hooded
> I do not know whether a man or a woman
> – But who is that on the other side of you?

'What the Thunder said' is the section where the Narrator comes nearest to contact with supernatural truth, and the choice of this episode from the end of St. Luke's gospel is particularly apt. It refers to the time when Christ has risen but the disciples believe he has gone from them forever. They are in the bleak, uncertain period of being without a God when, in his resurrected form, they encounter him on the road to Emmaus. They do not recognize him and think he is a stranger: 'their eyes were holden that they should not know him'. However, they talk, and only at the close – and just as he leaves them – do they recognize Christ for who he is:

And their eyes were opened, and they knew him; and he vanished out of their sight.

And they said to one another, Did not our heart burn within us, while he talked with us by the way, and while he opened to us the scriptures?

Mankind does not even recognize its saviour face to face.

Eliot, of course, deliberately compares the risen Christ to Frazer's Hanged God (see pp. 96–7). By choosing to do this here in the context of Christ's reappearance on the road to Emmaus, Eliot suggests that, even though the deity can be resurrected – and, hence, the Waste Land may be redeemed – man is blinded to the spiritual and cannot recognize his Redeemer. Because of his nature, man cannot have immediate and comforting access to Christ or the Hanged God. The world of the Waste Land is such that revelation, when it comes, is not fully recognized for what it is.

Shakespeare and the poetry of the English Renaissance

We have seen that the closing lines of *Gerontion* are a creative imitation of such Jacobean dramatists as Webster (see pp. 23–4). They are both exposition and poetry, both abstract and emotionally engaging, their effect – in Eliot's own words – 'a direct sensuous apprehension of thought, or a recreation of thought into feelings'. But the macabre elements in these plays also have an important place in *The Waste Land*. Webster, in particular, provided Eliot with lines which suggest the sinister that underlies life in all ages (see ll. 74, 114 and 407).

Eliot also made considerable use of another Jacobean playwright; Thomas Middleton. His admiration for him is clear in his discussion of the dramatist in *The Sacred Wood* (1929), where, while admitting that his subject has passages that are conventional and even turgid, he nonetheless places him next to Shakespeare among the dramatists of his time for his ability to catch 'permanent human feelings'. Writing of *Women Beware Women*, Eliot says: 'In this play Middleton shows his interest – more than any of his contemporaries – in innuendo and double meanings; and makes use of that game of chess, which he was to use more openly and directly for satire in that perfect piece of literary political art, *A Game at Chesse*.' This, of course, leads us directly to the second section of *The Waste Land*.

The game of chess in *Women Beware Women* takes place in the second Act of the play and is designed to beguile the mother of a girl who is being seduced. In other words, it is part of the sexual intrigue in 'what appears on the surface a conventional picture-palace Italian melodrama'. Sexual intrigue in a world lacking moral values, a world bizarre, neurotic, and overwrought, provides the tone both in Middleton's play and in the second section of *The Waste Land*. Indeed, the two works are charged with sexual violence, and Eliot's title here is meant to trigger in our memories Middleton's use of chess as a metaphor for the battle of vice and virtue, the transience of life and the sense of playing games with people's emotions. All these are present in the second section of Eliot's poem, while the 'innuendo and double meanings' are less a matter of sexual symbolism than of the breakdown of sex into loveless and non-procreative neurosis, into hints of violence, despair and spiritual death.

The women in the pub in the second part of this section also hint at extra-marital affairs and squalid intrigues, while making it clear that abortions have wrecked their looks and taken away whatever delights their love-making may have held. In the earlier section, even this degree of communication has broken down. The couple can only talk *at* each other. The violence is not that of rape and distraction as it is in Middleton, but rather of mental cruelty and incoherence, the modern world of vicious, private neurosis where a real game of chess may serve only as a distraction from the horror of life (see l. 137).

Eliot's use of the macabre elements in seventeenth-century literature is clear in his reference to Andrew Marvell's *To His Coy Mistress* in 'The Fire Sermon' (l. 196). As the Narrator sits huddled on the bank of the 'dull canal', what he hears at his back is not 'time's wingèd chariot hurrying near', but Sweeney (see pp. 22–3 and 81–2) going to a brothel, a place where he may, to follow Eliot's reference, see his woman's 'naked skin'. This obviously is not a matter of pleasure but rather of spiritual death akin to the sense of actual physical death suggested by Marvell.

Sweeney and Mrs Porter, the brothel-keeper, are then subsumed into Actaeon and Diana, at once demeaning the myth and reminding us of its sexual violence: the hunter Actaeon gazed on the goddess of chastity and, as a punishment, was metamorphosed into a stag, only to be killed by his own hounds. Once again we are reminded of the violence that surrounds Greek myths, particularly those concerning erotic love, which so obsessed Eliot at this period.

Of the other non-dramatic poets of the English Renaissance who also contribute to *The Waste Land*, Milton occurs at l. 98 with an ironic reference to Eden; but it is Spenser who provides the more telling allusions. His *Prothalamion* is a poem written to celebrate the forthcoming marriage of the two daughters of the Earl of Worcester. Its subjects are love, happy marriage and the power and beauty of London. These, clearly, are themes related to *The Waste Land*. In Eliot's poem, the Thames is a polluted river, corrupted like the rest of the City and associated in Eliot's mind with the tragedy surrounding the theft of the Rhinegold (see p. 126). In Spenser's poem, the Thames is a place of natural sexual joy and high culture, a place of order, marriage and celebration where the nymphs are 'lovely Daughters of the Flood' rather than secretaries out for a good time with the boss. It is against such lines as these that we are supposed to measure the modern world of squalor and meaningless sex. Their content again illustrates very clearly Eliot's technique of reference and contrast as a means of showing con-temporary social decline:

> And let fair Venus, that is queen of love,
> With her heart-quelling son upon you smile,
> Whose smile, they say, hath virtue to remove
> All love's dislike, and friendship's faulty guile
> For ever to assoil.
> Let endless peace your steadfast hearts accord,
> And blessed plenty wait upon your board,
> And let your bed with pleasures chaste abound,
> That fruitful issue may to you afford,
> Which may your foes confound,
> And make your joys rebound,
> Upon your bridal day, which is not long:
> Sweet Thames, run softly, till I end my song.

The most significant references from this period, however, are to Shakespeare. The opening of 'A Game of Chess', for example, is a parody of Enobarbus's speech in *Antony and Cleopatra*:

> The barge she sat in, like a burnish'd throne,
> Burn'd on the water: the poop was beaten gold;
> Purple the sails, and so perfumed that
> The winds were love-sick with them; the oars were silver,
> Which to the tune of flutes kept stroke, and made
> The water which they beat to follow faster,
> As amorous of their strokes. For her own person,
> It beggar'd all description: she did lie
> In her pavilion – cloth-of-gold of tissue –
> O'erpicturing that Venus where we see
> The fancy outwork nature. On each side her
> Stood pretty dimpled boys, like smiling Cupids,
> With divers-colour'd fans, whose wind did seem
> To glow the delicate cheeks which they did cool,
> And what they undid did.

The picture here is of the potent, fabulously luxurious queen of Egypt. The first line is clearly parodied by Eliot (l. 77), but notice also the detail of the Cupid (compare ll. 80–81). Later in the speech we are told that Cleopatra's 'strange invisible perfume' spreads out from the barge to the banks of the river. It helps to draw the people to behold this reincarnation of Venus (compare ll. 86–93). In Eliot's poem the perfume is suffocating, threatening. Finally, such is the lure of Cleopatra that Antony is left alone, 'whistling to th' air'. Even that element would have gone to have greeted the queen were it not that by so doing it would have left a vacuum behind it – and 'nature abhors a vacuum'. The man in the opening lines of 'A Game of Chess', of course, is similarly left alone – he is deserted in a moral and emotional vacuum, and, unlike Antony, cannot rouse himself to celebrate his love with a feast. The potency and sexual promise of Shakespeare's Cleopatra (albeit a promise that ended in destruction) is gloriously enhancing, the description of a wonder in nature; the woman in Eliot's poem is described through an imagery and syntax that ally her increasingly to the neurotic, the violent, and – with the further reference to Dido – to the ironically repeated idea of tragic love. There is no longer any grandeur in the tragedy. The words of Eliot's woman here are neither noble nor edifying. They are merely a reflection of her neurosis, the lowest common – and purely modern – denominator of the scene.

The brief reference to *Hamlet* at the close of 'A Game of Chess' (l. 172) is a particularly good example of how Eliot's use of seventeenth-century poetry heightens the sense of squalor in the modern world. Hamlet has been driven to the edges of sanity very largely by sexual intrigue: his mother's over-hasty marriage to her husband's murderer and their subsequent machinations over his affair with Ophelia. Hamlet, too, has his vision of a Waste Land, of an 'unweeded garden', but in his dangerous and fascinating melancholy there is a profound yet aristocratic sense of chaos and world-sorrow in a Denmark where values have collapsed, love is denied and self-questioning ends in neurosis. The Renaissance beauty and endless ambiguity of the play is, however, terribly out of place in this East End public house with its talk of abortions and squalid deceit.

The reference in l. 416 to *Coriolanus* – Eliot's favourite Shakespeare tragedy – is suggestive of tragic selfishness. Coriolanus, obsessed with his own honour and dignity, deserts to the enemies of Rome, only to find that he has no role beyond self-destructive violence when he is away from the city to whose service he is dedicated. This is the height of that solipsistic world to which Eliot refers us in his quotation from F. H. Bradley.

The most important series of Shakespearian references are to *The Tempest*. The reference which comes just after the typist's seduction by the house agent's clerk is perhaps the most useful one to start with (l. 257). After a parody of Goldsmith's lovely lyric from *The Vicar of Wakefield* in which we learn that:

> When lovely woman stoops to folly and
> Paces about her room again, alone,
> She smoothes her hair with automatic hand,
> And puts a record on the gramophone

the Narrator immediately thinks of the young Prince Ferdinand in *The Tempest*.

The Tempest was Shakespeare's last complete play, the culmination of his career and of the four 'romances' that close it. In all of these last works, love triumphs over chaos and the unnatural. The particular moment in *The Tempest* that Eliot here refers us to comes in the second scene of Act I where the young Prince Ferdinand – the embodiment of youthful courtly grace and love – believes that his father has been drowned. We see him wandering round the island on which he has been cast up and trying to find any of his companions who might have been saved. The island itself is ruled by the magician Prospero, whose fairy servant Ariel (invisible at this moment) guides the young prince onwards with his song. As he does so, he brings Ferdinand in sight of Prospero and his beautiful daughter, Miranda. The young couple, of course, fall in love. The whole is a moment of benevolent magic and great poetic charm underlined by the melancholy thought of Ferdinand's drowned father. As Ariel's first song ends, Ferdinand declares:

> Where should this music be? I' th' air or th' earth?
> It sounds no more; and sure it waits upon
> Some god o' th' island. Sitting on a bank,
> Weeping again the King my father's wreck,
> This music crept by me upon the waters,
> Allaying both their fury and my passion
> With its sweet air.

The contrast to *The Waste Land* is most effective. The Narrator, fishing in the 'dull canal', is led by no such sense of magic and kindly providence. He is moving in a sterile land. There is no hope of a redeeming love for him. Rather, he hears the music of the newly seduced typist, and memories of the corrupted Thames and modern sterility come to him.

And, naturally, Eliot draws a parallel between Ferdinand's drowned father and the drowned Phoenician sailor. Ariel's song beautifully describes the former:

> Full fathom five thy father lies;
>   Of his bones are coral made;
> Those are pearls that were his eyes;
>   Nothing of him that doth fade
> But doth suffer a sea-change
> Into something rich and strange.
> Sea-nymphs hourly ring his knell:
> (*Burden*) Ding-dong.
> Hark! Now I hear them – Ding-dong bell.

Here there is a metamorphosis into something beautiful and fantastic, the 'sea-change' which all the characters undergo in their symbolic drowning. In *The Tempest* (as in the fertility rites of the ancients, see pp. 95–6) the characters pass through a drowning eventually to emerge resurrected into a world of love and harmony. In *The Waste Land* this is not so. Phlebas only drowns and dies. The tides slowly pick his body away. It is this contrast between death followed by resurrection into a fuller life and mere 'death by drowning' that the anguished man in 'A Game of Chess' remembers (ll. 124–5), and Eliot's Notes refer us back to the moments of ecstasy in 'The Burial of the Dead':

> – Yet when we came back, late, from the hyacinth garden,
> Your arms full, and your hair wet, I could not
> Speak, and my eyes failed, I was neither
> Living nor dead, and I knew nothing,
> Looking into the heart of light, the silence.

Here is the love that could revive but fails to do so. It has ended in death – either spiritual or actual – and the broken Narrator, consulting Madame Sosostris, can only partially recapture it through the card of 'the drowned Phoenician Sailor' whose death he is told he should fear.

The web of allusion is here at its most finely meshed. We have, on the one hand, *The Tempest* with its love and benevolent magic, its drownings and 'sea-change' into fuller life, and, on the other, the comparison to the Narrator, whose love has failed and who wanders the corrupt modern world, saddened by what he sees and wracked by memories of his affair. This, because it was insufficient, places him in a Waste Land. Drowning has ended only in death. There is no resurrection of sexual passion and religious faith, for they are no longer at one. Instead of the redemption offered by Shakespeare and the fertility myths, there is only the glimpse of the debased tradition of such things on Madame Sosostris's cards, and she tells her querent to fear the very thing that could lead to the Waste Land being restored. Since such salvation cannot be, the Narrator sits by the 'dull canal', an embodiment of the Fisher King himself, whose deep psychic wound brings to the world destruction, despair, drought and confusion. The great myths and life-enhancing poetry of the past are brought together only to show how sterile the present world is – a Waste Land.

Afterword

The Waste Land is a central work of modernism. It takes its place beside Picasso's *Les Demoiselles d'Avignon*, Stravinsky's *The Rite of Spring* and Joyce's *Ulysses*. Like them, it is both a culmination of much that had gone before and a radical new departure. It is almost the definition of such masterpieces that they generate a new syntax from age-old pre-occupations. And their language, once learnt, is permanently enriching. Many readers have found in *The Waste Land* an expression of their own fears or discovered in it their own disillusion. But Eliot himself was chary of accepting this tribute. He claimed at first that *The Waste Land* was a purely personal work, but later came to realize that others found that it spoke for them. Now the poem must be seen as a seminal part of our heritage. Several qualities ensure it this status: among them, the passion of its analysis and its integrity as a work of art. The first can be known only when the poem is thoroughly familiar – when we have got it in our bones. The second is a matter for analysis, but is, too, a part of the effect. Yet if one were to single out what is most compelling about *The Waste Land*, it would perhaps be its drama, its desperate engagement with the modern world. It is a curious reflection that we are as far removed from it in time as Eliot was from Baudelaire. Between these two poets lay the abyss of the First World War and the collapse of certainties. Between us and *The Waste Land* lies another world war and more massive means of destruction. The abyss has not been bridged. It has widened. However, *The Waste Land* still has the power to make us look at such things afresh, though, by a nice irony, we have institutionalized the poem so that it, too, is now one of the fragments to shore against our own ruins.

Bibliography

Editions

The Complete Poems and Plays of T. S. Eliot, Faber and Faber, 1969.

Collected Poems, 1909–1962, by T. S. Eliot, Faber and Faber, 1974.

T. S. Eliot: 'The Waste Land': A Facsimile and Transcript of the Original Drafts, Including the Annotations of Ezra Pound, ed. Valerie Eliot, Faber and Faber, 1971.

The Sacred Wood: Essays on Poetry and Criticism, Methuen, 1950.

Selected Essays, Faber and Faber, 1951.

On Poetry and Poets, Faber and Faber, 1957.

The Use of Poetry and the Use of Criticism, Faber and Faber, 1964.

For Lancelot Andrewes: Essays on Style and Order, Faber and Faber, 1970.

To Criticize the Critic and Other Writings, Faber and Faber, 1978.

Books on Eliot or containing important discussions of *The Waste Land*

ALVAREZ, A. *The Shaping Spirit*, Chatto and Windus, 1958.

BRADBROOK, M. C. *T. S. Eliot* (Writers and their Work), Longmans for the British Council, 1965.

BRADBROOK, M. C. *T. S. Eliot: The Making of 'The Waste Land'*, Longmans for the British Council, 1972

BROOKS, CLEANTH, *Modern Poetry and the Tradition*, University of North Carolina Press, 1939.

COX, C. B. and ARNOLD P. HINCHLIFFE (eds.) *T. S. Eliot: 'The Waste Land': A Casebook*, Macmillan, 1968.

EMPSON, WILLIAM, *Seven Types of Ambiguity*, Chatto and Windus, 1930.

FRYE, NORTHROP, *T. S. Eliot*, Oliver and Boyd, 1963.

GARDNER, HELEN, *The Art of T. S. Eliot*, Dutton, 1949.

GORDON, LYNDALL, *Eliot's Early Years*, Oxford University Press, 1977.

KENNER, HUGH, *The Invisible Poet: T. S. Eliot*, Methuen, 1959.

LEAVIS, F. R., *New Bearings in English Poetry*, Chatto and Windus, 1932.

MARTIN, G. (ed.) *Eliot in Perspective*, Macmillan, 1970.

MATTHIESSEN, F. O., *The Achievement of T. S. Eliot*, Oxford University Press, 1958.

RICHARDS, I. A, *Principles of Literary Criticism*, Harcourt, Brace and World, Inc., 1948.

SPENDER, STEPHEN, *Eliot* (Fontana Modern Masters), Fontana, 1977.
STEAD, C. F. *The New Poetic*, Hutchinson, 1964.
WILSON, EDMUND. *Axel's Castle: A Study in the Imaginative Literature of 1870–1930*, Fontana Library, 1961.